How to Use
History Pockets

*I*n *History Pockets—Explorers of North America,* the journeys of 10 famous adventurers are highlighted. The engaging activities are stored in labeled pockets and bound into a decorative cover. Students will be proud to see their accumulated projects presented all together. At the end of the book, evaluation sheets have been added for teacher use.

Make a Pocket

1. Use a 12" x 18" (30.5 x 45.5 cm) piece of construction paper for each pocket. Fold up 6" (15 cm) to make a 12" (30.5 cm) square.

2. Staple the right side of each pocket closed.

3. Punch two or three holes in the left side of each pocket.

Assemble the Pocket Book

1. Reproduce the cover illustration on page 3 for each student.

2. Direct students to color and cut out the illustration and glue it onto a 12" (30.5 cm) square of construction paper to make the cover.

3. Punch two or three holes in the left side of the cover.

4. Fasten the cover and the pockets together. You might use string, ribbon, twine, raffia, or binder rings.

Every Pocket Has...

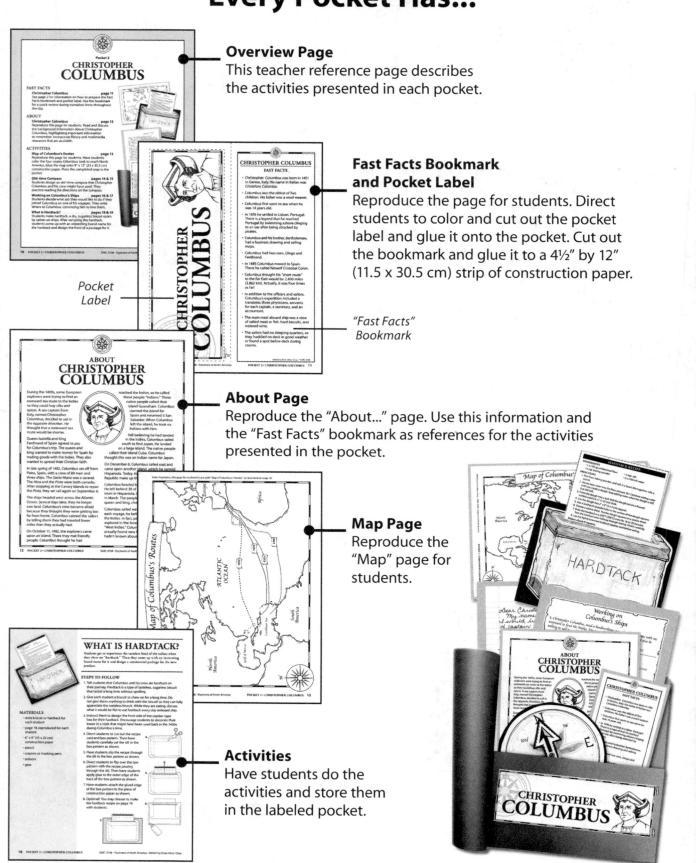

Overview Page
This teacher reference page describes the activities presented in each pocket.

Pocket Label

Fast Facts Bookmark and Pocket Label
Reproduce the page for students. Direct students to color and cut out the pocket label and glue it onto the pocket. Cut out the bookmark and glue it to a 4½" by 12" (11.5 x 30.5 cm) strip of construction paper.

"Fast Facts" Bookmark

About Page
Reproduce the "About..." page. Use this information and the "Fast Facts" bookmark as references for the activities presented in the pocket.

Map Page
Reproduce the "Map" page for students.

Activities
Have students do the activities and store them in the labeled pocket.

EMC 3708 • Explorers of North America • ©2003 by Evan-Moor Corp.

Note: Reproduce this cover for students to color, cut out, and glue to the cover of their Explorers of North America book.

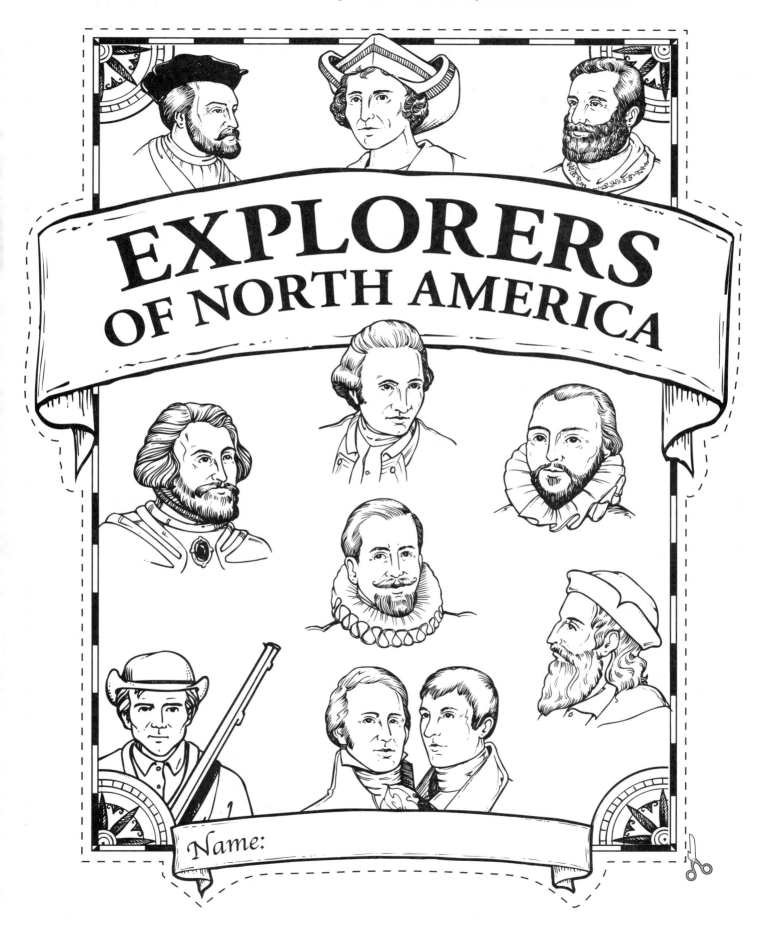

EXPLORERS
OF NORTH AMERICA

Name:

Pocket 1 • INTRODUCTION TO

EXPLORERS
OF NORTH AMERICA

FAST FACTS

Explorers of North America . . . . **page 5**
See page 2 for information on how to prepare the Fast Facts bookmark and pocket label. Use the bookmark for a quick review during transition times throughout the day.

ABOUT

Explorers of North America . . . . **page 6**
Reproduce this page for students. Read and discuss the background information about explorers of North America, highlighting important information to remember. Incorporate library and multimedia resources that are available.

ACTIVITIES

Map of 10 Explorers' Routes . . . . **page 7**
Reproduce this page for students. Have students study the routes of the 10 explorers that are on this map. Glue the map onto 9" x 12" (23 x 30.5 cm) construction paper. Have students save this map in Pocket 1, and as each new explorer is studied, they may look back for review.

Time Line of 10 Explorers . . . . **pages 8 & 9**
As each of the 10 explorers is studied, students color the picture of the explorer. Have students store the time line in Pocket 1.

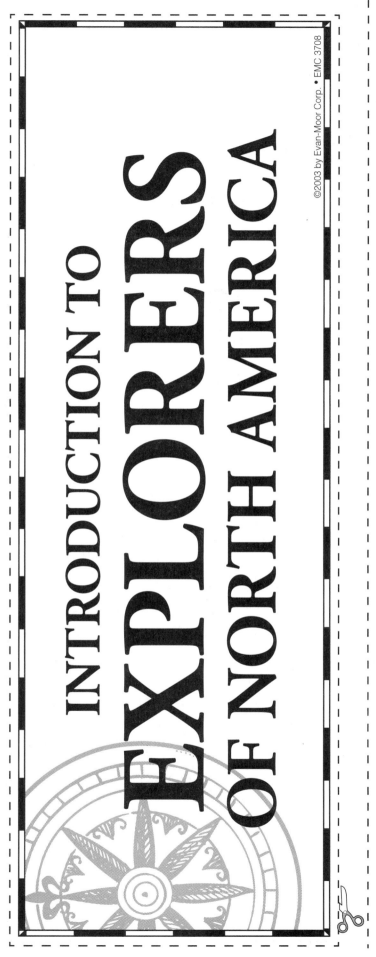

INTRODUCTION TO

EXPLORERS
OF NORTH AMERICA

EXPLORERS
OF NORTH AMERICA

FAST FACTS

- During the 1400s and 1500s, explorers had a difficult time finding a crew because some men thought the world was flat and they would fall off the edge of the earth.

- Many maps of the 1400s and 1500s showed Europe in the center, surrounded by oceans full of sea monsters waiting to devour sailors.

- In 1416 Prince Henry of Portugal founded a navigational school in Sagres, Portugal, that sailors attended.

- The Chinese actually discovered the first simple compass 2,000 years ago.

- The first kind of telescope was invented at the same time in England, Italy, and Holland. Explorers of the 1600s found this telescope vital for sighting landmarks at great distances.

- Sailors had to go months without fresh foods, so they lacked vitamin C. This vitamin C deficiency caused a terrible disease called scurvy. Scurvy caused nausea, weakness, loss of hair and teeth, and then death. More sailors died of scurvy than any other cause.

- Sailors spent many months at sea without sighting land. They would sometimes plan to kill the captain and turn back. This was called mutiny, and it was the worst crime. The penalty was death.

ABOUT
EXPLORERS
OF NORTH AMERICA

In the 1400s most Europeans knew little about the world outside of their own villages. Educated people knew of three continents—Europe, Africa, and Asia. They knew there were new lands to be discovered across the oceans.

The Europeans had discovered that new navigational tools would help them find their way across oceans. The magnetic compass indicated north, south, east, and west. The cross staff measured the distance between the horizon and the North Star to find latitude.

Europeans had learned about an Arab ship called the caravel. It had a rudder for steering. It also had triangular sails called lateens that let the ship sail in any direction. Older square-rigged sails let the ship sail only with the wind. Portuguese shipbuilders borrowed ideas from the caravel and created a larger, stronger ship called a carrack.

Europeans had several reasons for exploring new lands. They wanted to spread their Christian faith and expand their countries by owning new lands.

Another important reason for exploration was trade. Europeans found out that Arabs bought fine silks, spices, and perfumes from eastern Asia. The Europeans wanted these goods, so they bought Asian goods through the Arabs but were charged high prices.

The Europeans decided to find their own route to eastern Asia so they could buy these goods for cheaper prices. At the time, Europeans called this part of Asia "the Indies."

In 1271 an Italian merchant named Marco Polo traveled east by land and reached the Indies four years later. Polo later returned to Europe and explained that part of the Indies borders an ocean. Europeans started looking for ways to reach the Indies by water. Sailing would be quicker than by land, and the ships could carry plenty of goods.

In the 1400s Prince Henry of Portugal figured out that ships could sail east to reach the Indies. Prince Henry paid sailing crews to find the route, but his men didn't get farther than the western coast of Africa.

In 1488 Bartolomeu Dias of Portugal sailed around the tip of Africa. He did not make it to the Indies. The exploration race was on.

Note: Reproduce this page for students to use with "Map of 10 Explorers' Routes," as described on page 4.

Map of 10 Explorers' Routes
Europe
Africa
ATLANTIC OCEAN
Cook
Hudson
Cabot
Cartier
Columbus
South America
Lewis & Clark
Boone
Cortes
Drake
Powell
North America
PACIFIC OCEAN
ARCTIC OCEAN
Australia
Cook
INDIAN OCEAN
Asia
N
Note: One representative route from each explorer has been used for this reference map.

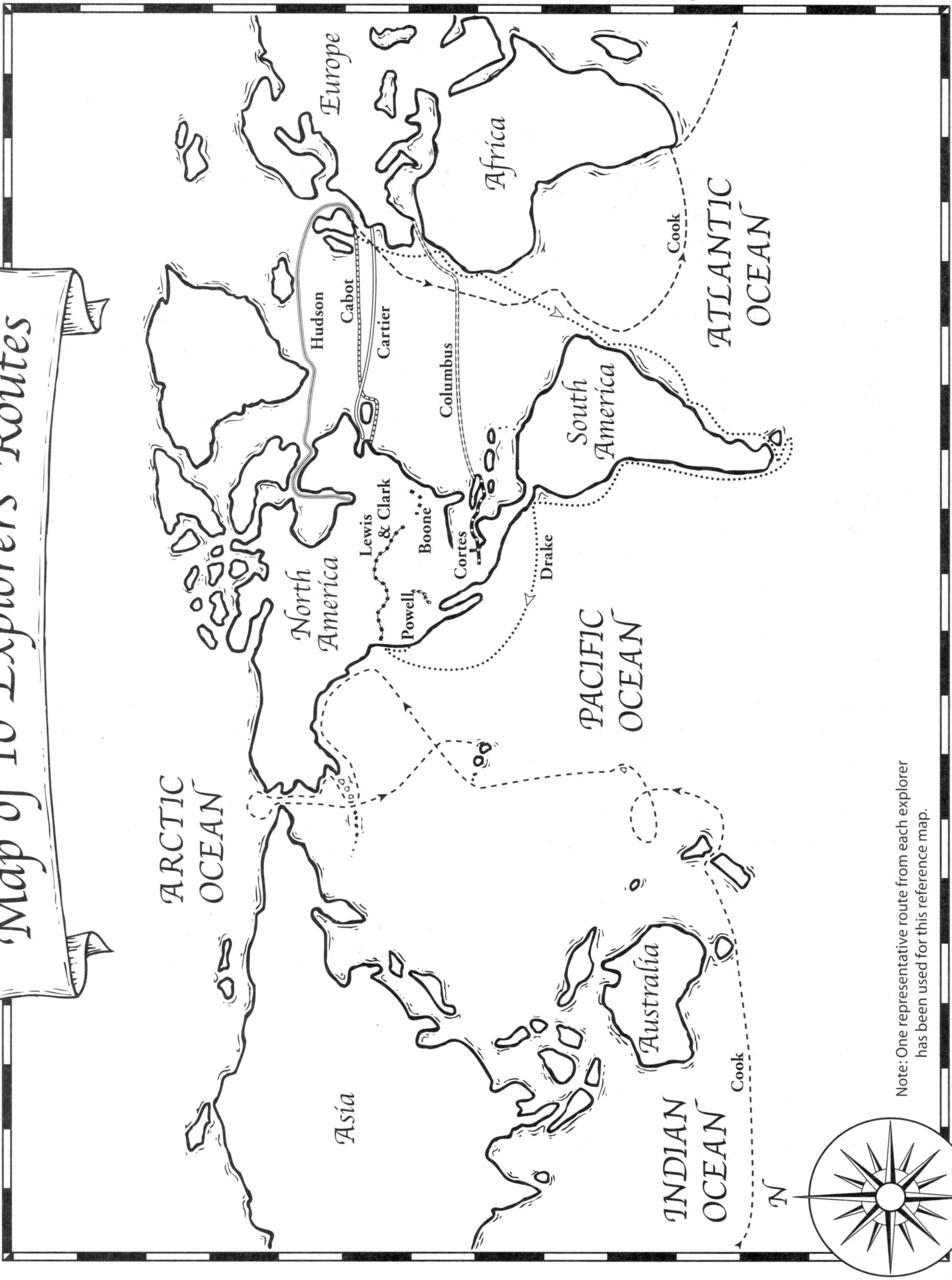

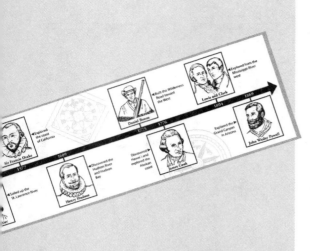

TIME LINE OF 10 EXPLORERS

As an ongoing activity, students first make a time line for 10 explorers of North America. They color the pictures of the explorers as each one of them is studied.

STEPS TO FOLLOW

1. Discuss with students that there were many explorers of North America. This unit focuses on 10 of them. Tell them the time they will study is from the 1400s to the 1800s. They will do this by keeping a time line of 10 explorers of North America.

2. Have students cut apart the three time line panels on pages 8 and 9.

3. Direct students to glue or staple the three panels together to make the time line. Have them fold the time line so the title is showing.

4. As each explorer is studied, students will color his picture.

5. Remind students to store the folded time line in Pocket 1.

MATERIALS

• pages 8 (bottom half) and 9, reproduced for each student
• scissors
• glue
• stapler
• colored pencils

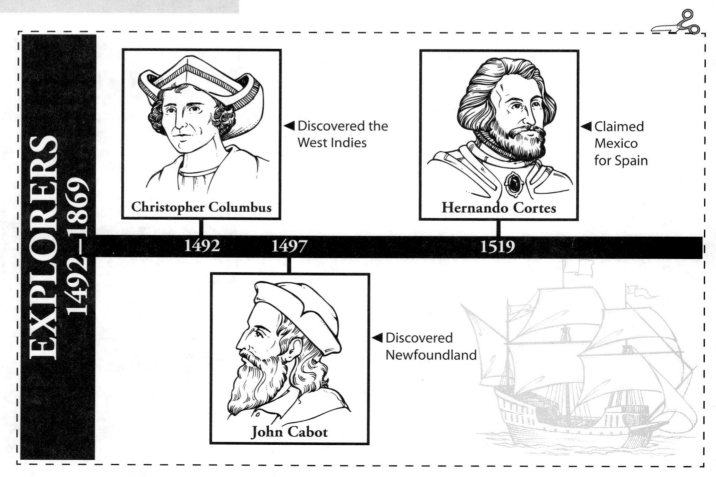

EXPLORERS 1492–1869

Christopher Columbus ◄ Discovered the West Indies

Hernando Cortes ◄ Claimed Mexico for Spain

John Cabot ◄ Discovered Newfoundland

1492   1497   1519

TIME LINE OF 10 EXPLORERS

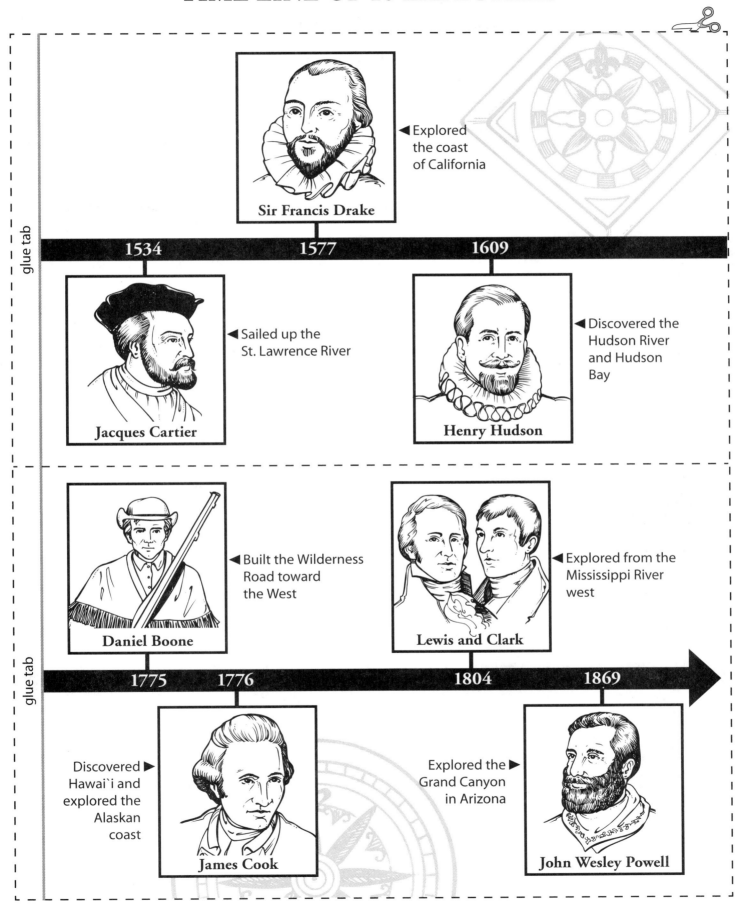

Sir Francis Drake

◀ Explored the coast of California

1534   1577   1609

Jacques Cartier

◀ Sailed up the St. Lawrence River

Henry Hudson

◀ Discovered the Hudson River and Hudson Bay

Daniel Boone

◀ Built the Wilderness Road toward the West

Lewis and Clark

◀ Explored from the Mississippi River west

1775   1776   1804   1869

Discovered Hawai`i and explored the Alaskan coast ▶

James Cook

Explored the Grand Canyon in Arizona ▶

John Wesley Powell

glue tab

glue tab

Pocket 2

CHRISTOPHER COLUMBUS

FAST FACTS

Christopher Columbus. . . . .
See page 2 for information on how to prepare the Fast
Facts bookmark and pocket label. Use the bookmark
for a quick review during transition times throughout
the day.

ABOUT

Christopher Columbus. . . . .
Reproduce this page for students. Read and discuss
the background information about Christopher
Columbus, highlighting important information
to remember. Incorporate library and multimedia
resources that are available.

ACTIVITIES

Map of Columbus's Routes . . . .
Reproduce this page for students. Have students
color the four routes Columbus took to reach North
America. Glue the map onto 9" x 12" (23 x 30.5 cm)
construction paper. Place the completed map in the
pocket.

Old-time Compass . . . .
Students design an old-time compass that Christopher
Columbus and his crew might have used. They
practice reading the directions on the compass.

Working on Columbus's Ships . . . .
Students decide what job they would like to do if they
joined Columbus on one of his voyages. They write
letters to Columbus, convincing him to hire them.

What Is Hardtack? . . . .
Students make hardtack, a dry, sugarless biscuit eaten
by sailors on ships. After sampling the hardtack,
students come up with an interesting brand name for
the hardtack and design the front of a package for it.

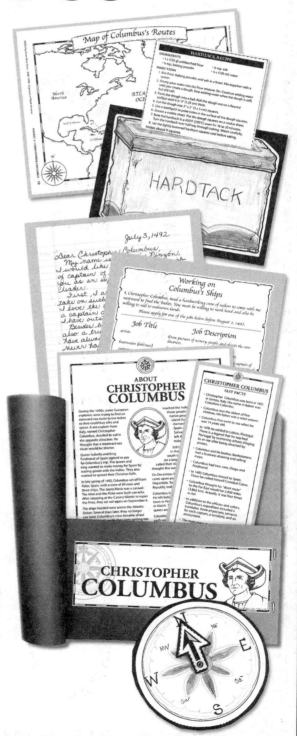

     EMC 3708 • Explorers of North America • ©2003 by Evan-Moor Corp.

CHRISTOPHER COLUMBUS

CHRISTOPHER COLUMBUS

FAST FACTS

- Christopher Columbus was born in 1451 in Genoa, Italy. His name in Italian was Cristoforo Colombo.

- Columbus was the oldest of five children. His father was a wool weaver.

- Columbus first went to sea when he was 14 years old.

- In 1476 he settled in Lisbon, Portugal. There is a legend that he reached Portugal by swimming ashore clinging to an oar after being attacked by pirates.

- Columbus and his brother, Bartholomew, had a business drawing and selling maps.

- Columbus had two sons, Diego and Ferdinand.

- In 1485 Columbus moved to Spain. There he called himself Cristobal Colon.

- Columbus thought his "short route" to the Far East would be 2,400 miles (3,862 km). Actually, it was four times as far!

- In addition to the officers and sailors, Columbus's expedition included a translator, three physicians, servants for each captain, a secretary, and an accountant.

- The main meal aboard ship was a stew of salted meat or fish, hard biscuits, and watered wine.

- The sailors had no sleeping quarters, so they huddled on deck in good weather or found a spot below deck during storms.

ABOUT
CHRISTOPHER COLUMBUS

During the 1400s, some European explorers were trying to find an eastward sea route to the Indies so they could buy silks and spices. A sea captain from Italy, named Christopher Columbus, decided to sail in the opposite direction. He thought that a westward sea route would be shorter.

Queen Isabella and King Ferdinand of Spain agreed to pay for Columbus's trip. The queen and king wanted to make money for Spain by trading goods with the Indies. They also wanted to spread their Christian faith.

In late spring of 1492, Columbus set off from Palos, Spain, with a crew of 89 men and three ships. The *Santa Maria* was a caravel. The *Nina* and the *Pinta* were both carracks. After stopping at the Canary Islands to repair the *Pinta*, they set sail again on September 6.

The ships headed west across the Atlantic Ocean. Several days later, they no longer saw land. Columbus's crew became afraid because they thought they were getting too far from home. Columbus calmed the sailors by telling them they had traveled fewer miles than they actually had.

On October 11, 1492, the explorers came upon an island. There they met friendly people. Columbus thought he had reached the Indies, so he called these people "Indians." These native people called their island Guanahani. Columbus claimed the island for Spain and renamed it San Salvador. When Columbus left the island, he took six Indians with him.

Still believing he had landed in the Indies, Columbus sailed south to find Japan. He landed on a large island. The native people called their island Cuba. Columbus thought this was an Indian name for Japan.

On December 6, Columbus sailed east and came upon another island, which he named Hispaniola. Today, Haiti and the Dominican Republic make up this island.

Columbus headed back to Spain in January. He left behind 39 of his own men to set up a town in Hispaniola. Columbus reached Spain in March. The people of Spain, as well as the queen and king, cheered him.

Columbus sailed west three more times. On each voyage, he believed he had reached the Indies. In fact, part of the area he explored in the Americas is still called the "West Indies." Columbus never knew he had actually found new lands that Europeans hadn't known about.

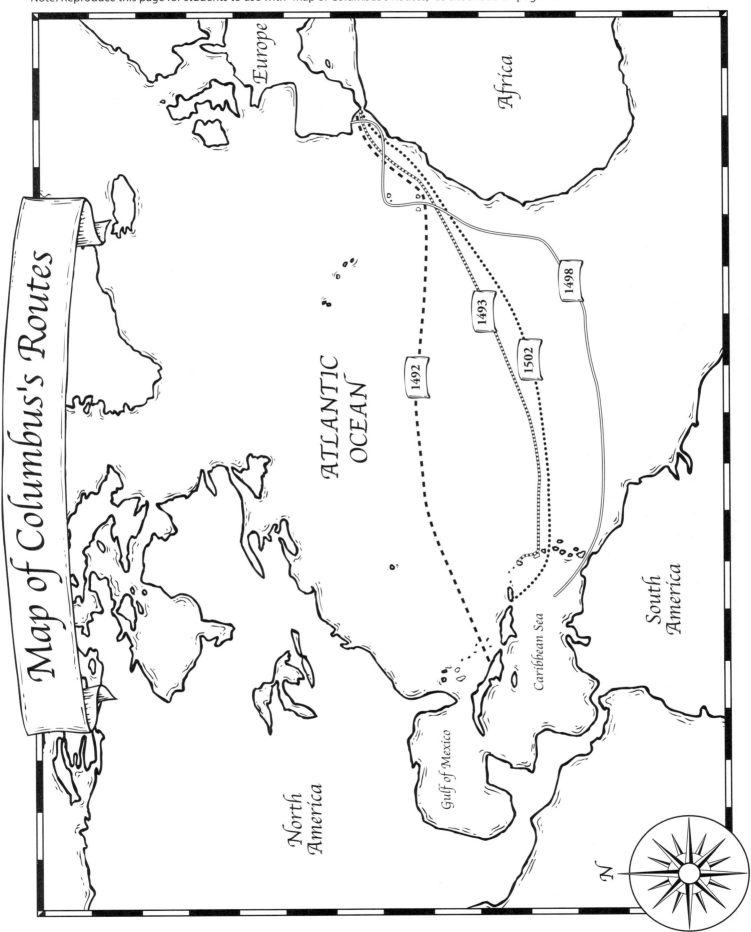

Map of Columbus's Routes

Europe

Africa

ATLANTIC OCEAN

1498

1493

1502

1492

North America

Gulf of Mexico

Caribbean Sea

South America

N

MATERIALS

- page 15, reproduced for each student
- colored pencils
- scissors
- 9" x 12" (23 x 30.5 cm) colored construction paper
- glue
- paper fastener

OLD-TIME COMPASS

Students can design their own old-time compasses that Christopher Columbus and his crew might have used. They can practice reading the directions on the compass.

STEPS TO FOLLOW

1. Explain to students that during Columbus's day, compasses were often decorated with fancy designs. Discuss the illustrations of old-time compasses at the bottom of the student page. Talk about compass directions—north, south, east, and west—and where they are located on the compass.

2. Have them draw designs on their copies of the compass face on page 15 using colored pencils. They should add "N," "S," "E," and "W" to their compasses in a style of lettering they choose. North should appear at the top of the compass. They should also decorate and color the direction arrow at the bottom of the page.

3. Direct students to cut out the compass and glue it to the construction paper.

4. Next, have students cut out the direction arrow and glue it to construction paper. They poke a hole in the arrow and attach it to the center of the compass with a paper fastener.

5. Ask students to move the arrows on their compasses to indicate the primary directions: north, south, east, and west.

6. Teach them about intermediate directions: northeast, northwest, southeast, and southwest. Have them find these intermediate directions on the compasses.

OLD-TIME COMPASS DESIGN

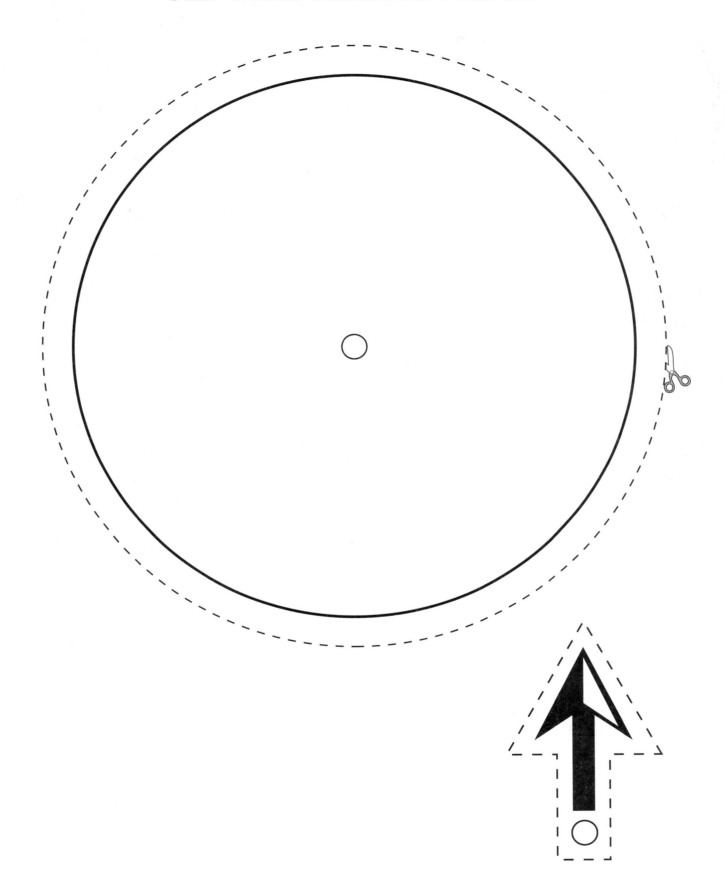

MATERIALS

- page 17, reproduced for each student
- 9" x 12" (23 x 30.5 cm) construction paper
- pencil
- writing paper

WORKING ON COLUMBUS'S SHIPS

Students have the opportunity to decide what job they would like to do if they sailed aboard one of Columbus's three ships. They then write letters to Columbus, stating why they think they should be hired to do their chosen jobs.

STEPS TO FOLLOW

1. Ask students to pretend it is 1492. Have them imagine they are walking along a road in the town of Palos. Palos is located in southern Spain, along the Atlantic coast. In a nearby harbor, they notice three brand-new wooden ships they have never seen before. People are busy working on the ships and filling them with supplies. Your students walk farther along and stop to read a sign that has been posted on a building. It's a job announcement written by Christopher Columbus.

2. Pass out copies of the job announcement to each student. Explain that these are examples of jobs that people might have done on an explorer's sailing ship. Read the list with your students. Have students decide what talents and abilities a person would need to perform the job.

3. Have students decide which of the jobs on the list they would most like to do if they lived back in Columbus's time.

4. When students have selected their jobs, direct them to write letters to Columbus, convincing him to hire them for their chosen jobs. They will need to include a list of what talents— real or imaginary—they have that would help them be the best person for the job. They should also write about why they would be willing to leave the comfort of home in Spain to sail to unknown lands.

5. Direct students to mount the letters and page 17 back to back on construction paper.

6. Invite students to share their letters with the class.

Working on Columbus's Ships

I, Christopher Columbus, need a hardworking crew of sailors to come with me westward to find the Indies. You must be willing to work hard and also be willing to sail to unknown lands.

Please apply for one of the jobs below before August 3, 1492.

Job Title	Job Description
artists	Draw pictures of scenery, people, and objects the crew discovers.
boatswains (boh'zuns)	In charge of sails, rope, rigging, and anchors.
captains	Leaders of the ships. I, Columbus, will be the captain of the Santa Maria. But I need two people to be captains of the Nina and Pinta.
carpenters	Repair the ship and build new ones when needed.
cooks	Prepare the food.
doctors	Help people when they are sick or hurt.
first mate	Carries out the captain's orders.
cleaning persons	Keep the boat clean and mop the floors.
mapmakers	Draw up maps of the lands discovered.
musicians	Play instruments and sing with the crew.
officers	Help the captain navigate the ship and make decisions.
sailmakers	Mend the sails and repair the ropes.
writers	Help the captain keep his ship's log, write messages, and write about what happens on the trip.
priests	In charge of religious events and services.
ship's boy or girl	Helps other people on the ship.
stewards	Look after the food and equipment stored on the ship.

WHAT IS HARDTACK?

Students get to experience the tasteless food of the sailors when they chew on "hardtack." Then they come up with an interesting brand name for it and design a commercial package for the new product.

MATERIALS

- stale biscuit or hardtack for each student
- page 19, reproduced for each student
- 6" x 9" (15 x 23 cm) construction paper
- pencil
- crayons or marking pens
- scissors
- glue

STEPS TO FOLLOW

1. Tell students that Columbus and his crew ate hardtack on their journey. Hardtack is a type of tasteless, sugarless biscuit that lasted a long time without spoiling.

2. Give each student a biscuit to chew on for a long time. Do not give them anything to drink with the biscuit so they can fully appreciate the tasteless biscuit. While they are eating, discuss what it would be like to eat hardtack every day onboard ship.

3. Instruct them to design the front side of the cracker-type box for their hardtack. Encourage students to decorate their boxes in a style that might have been used back in the 1400s during Columbus's time.

4. Direct students to cut out the recipe card and box pattern. Then have students carefully cut the slit in the box pattern as shown.

5. Have students slip the recipe through the slit in the box pattern as shown.

6. Direct students to flip over the box pattern with the recipe passing through the slit. Then have students apply glue to the outer edge of the back of the box pattern as shown.

7. Have students attach the glued edge of the box pattern to the piece of construction paper as shown.

8. Optional: You may choose to make the hardtack recipe on page 19 with students.

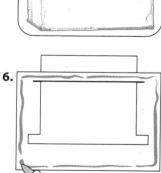

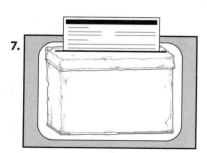

HARDTACK RECIPE

INGREDIENTS
- 1 c (125 g) unbleached flour
- ½ tsp. baking powder
- ⅛ tsp. salt
- ½ c (120 ml) water

DIRECTIONS

1. Mix flour, baking powder, and salt in a bowl. Mix together with a spoon.
2. Slowly pour water into the flour mixture. Stir. Continue adding water until you create a dough. Stop adding water when the dough is stiff, but still soft.
3. Form the dough into a ball. Roll the dough out on a floured surface until it is ½" (1.25 cm) thick.
4. Cut the dough into 2" x 2" (5 x 5 cm) squares.
5. Use a toothpick to poke holes in the surface of the dough squares.
6. Grease a cookie sheet. Put the dough squares on a cookie sheet.
7. Bake the hardtack in a 450°F (230°C) oven for 16 to 20 minutes. Turn the hardtack over halfway through baking. Watch carefully.
8. Let the lightly browned hardtack squares cool before eating.

Makes about 9 squares.

(cut to make slit)

JOHN CABOT

FAST FACTS

See page 2 for information on how to prepare the Fast Facts bookmark and pocket label. Use the bookmark for a quick review during transition times throughout the day.

ABOUT

Reproduce this page for students. Read and discuss the background information about John Cabot, highlighting important information to remember. Incorporate library and multimedia resources that are available.

ACTIVITIES

Reproduce this page for students. Have students color Cabot's 1497 exploration route. Glue the map onto 9" x 12" (23 x 30.5 cm) construction paper. Place the completed map in the pocket.

Shoals are shallow areas in the ocean that are full of ocean life. Students illustrate their own shoal and add pictures to it.

Students find a westerly sea route to the Indies (eastern Asia) from Europe that Cabot could have taken had he known America was in the way.

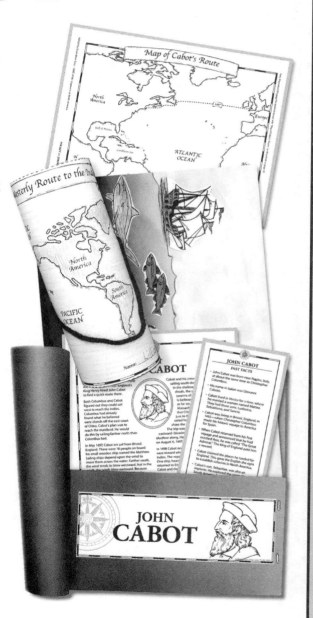

JOHN CABOT

FAST FACTS

- John Cabot was born near Naples, Italy, at about the same time as Christopher Columbus.

- His name in Italian was Giovanni Caboto.

- Cabot lived in Venice for a time, where he married a woman named Mattea. They had three sons: Ludovico, Sebastiano, and Sancio.

- Cabot was living in Bristol, England, in 1492—when Christopher Columbus made his historic voyage to America for Spain.

- When Cabot returned from his first voyage and announced that he had reached Asia, he was called "The Great Admiral." The king of England paid him a reward.

- Cabot claimed the places he landed for England. This gave the English the right to establish colonies in North America.

- Cabot's son, Sebastian, was also an explorer. He explored the coast of South America for Portugal.

- Cabot's son, Sancio, died with him during the unsuccessful voyage of 1498.

ABOUT
JOHN CABOT

Like Spain, England wanted to trade with the Indies. In 1497 England's King Henry hired John Cabot to find a quick route there.

Both Columbus and Cabot figured out they could sail west to reach the Indies. Columbus had already found what he believed were islands off the east coast of China. Cabot's plan was to reach the mainland. He would do this by sailing farther north than Columbus had.

In May 1497, Cabot set sail from Bristol, England. There were 18 people on board his small wooden ship named the *Matthew*. Sailing ships depend upon the wind to move them across the water. Farther south, the wind tends to blow westward, but in the north, the winds blow eastward. Because Cabot was sailing westward against the wind, his ship sailed slowly.

Several weeks later, a sailor saw a seagull. They sailed toward a pine-covered coastline. When Cabot reached the shore, he claimed the land for England. He named it New Found Land—or Newfoundland. Cabot thought he had landed in the northeast part of Asia.

Cabot and his crew continued sailing south down the coast. In the shallow waters, called shoals, the sailors found swarms of codfish. Cabot is believed to have sailed as far south as Boston, Massachusetts. He was sure that China and Japan were just to the south. Cabot sailed home for England to share the news of his discoveries. The trip was quicker because the eastward-blowing winds pushed the *Matthew* along. He reached Bristol, England, on August 6, 1497.

In 1498 Cabot once again sailed five ships west toward what he still thought was the Indies. The voyage is an historical mystery. One ship, heavily damaged by storms, returned to England. What happened to Cabot and the other four ships is unknown.

Like Christopher Columbus, John Cabot never realized his mistake. Instead of reaching the Indies, the two European explorers had landed upon a new continent.

EMC 3708 • Explorers of North America •©2003 by Evan-Moor Corp.

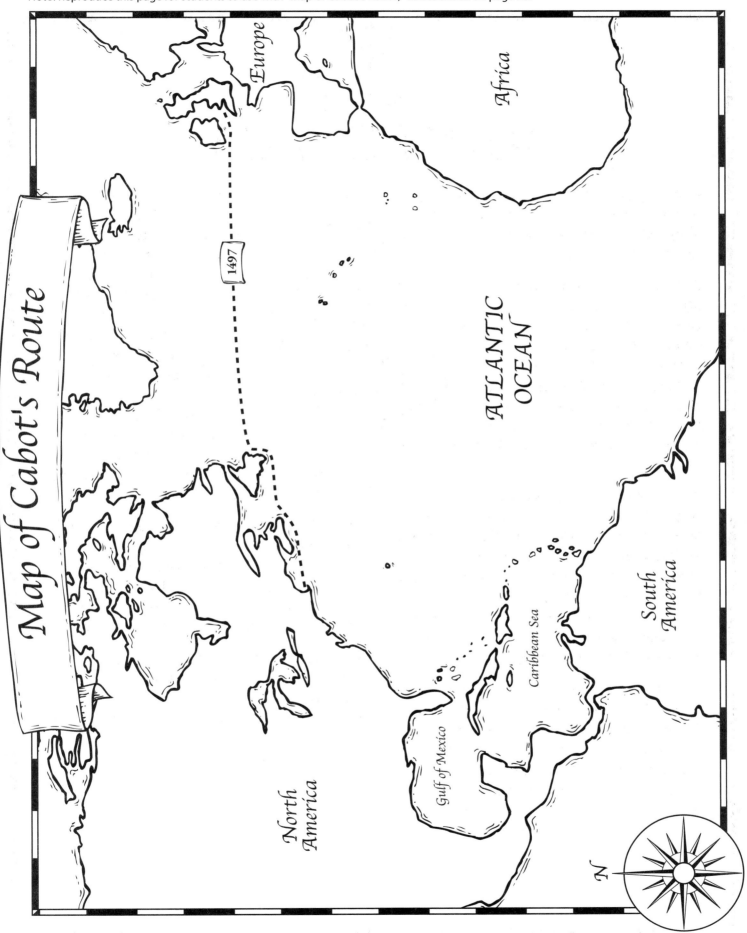

Map of Cabot's Route

1497

Europe

Africa

ATLANTIC OCEAN

North America

Gulf of Mexico

Caribbean Sea

South America

N

SHOAL PICTURES

Students illustrate a shoal and add pictures to it.

Share with Students

John Cabot fished for cod in shoals when he was sailing off the coast of Newfoundland. Shoals are shallow areas in the ocean created by the ocean floor coming near the surface. Because they are shallow, sunlight reaches the bottom of the shoal. Normally, the ocean is so deep that lower levels of the ocean are totally black. In a shoal, light warms the water and allows plants to grow. Swarms of codfish, tuna, mackerel, dolphins, whales, and underwater plants thrive in shoals. Today, shoals are mapped and are popular places to fish at sea.

MATERIALS

- page 25, reproduced for each student
- 12" x 18" (30.5 x 45.5 cm) white construction paper
- black crayon
- watercolor paints and brush
- crayons or marking pens
- glue

STEPS TO FOLLOW

1. Read the information about shoals to students. Show pictures of shoals in the ocean, if available.

2. Tell students that they are to make pictures of shoals.

3. On the construction paper, have them use the black crayon to draw a cross-sectional view of a shoal in the middle of the ocean. Then they watercolor the ocean floor below the shoal a brown or gray color. The ocean water itself is a bluish color, and the sky is a paler blue color. Let the painting dry.

4. Have students color Cabot's ship, and the animal- and plant-life pictures on page 25. Then they cut them out and glue them onto their watercolor pictures.

5. Optional: You may choose to have students write a short paragraph about a shoal to add to the picture.

EMC 3708 • Explorers of North America • ©2003 by Evan-Moor Corp.

SHOAL PICTURES

FINDING A WESTERLY ROUTE TO THE INDIES

Students find a westerly sea route from England to the Indies (eastern Asia) that Cabot could have taken had he known America was in the way.

MATERIALS

- page 27, reproduced for each student
- two paper clips per student
- scissors
- glue
- yarn

MAKING THE CYLINDER MAP

1. Cut out the map and roll the map back to form a cylinder map.

2. Tuck the tabbed end under the opposite shorter end.

3. Slip one paper clip over the top edge of the cylinder and another over the bottom.

USING THE CYLINDER MAP

1. Locate England and the Indies on the cylinder map.

2. Ask students which direction they would go in if they were going west (to the left).

3. Tell them to study their maps and find a westerly sea route from England all the way to the Indies. They will have to figure out the best way to "sail" around America. (Most will figure out that they must sail south around the lower tip of South America, although some students might choose a route above North America.)

4. Once they have decided on a route, have them carefully take the paper clips off the map to make it flat again, and instruct them to trace the route with a line of glue and cover the glue with a long piece of yarn.

5. Let the glue dry completely.

6. Discuss their discoveries. For those who found the route around the southern tip of South America, explain that this is the same route that Magellan made in 1520, when he sailed west from Europe to the Indies. For those who chose the route above North America, tell them that this route is called the Northwest Passage, and they will be finding out about several explorers who looked for this passage.

EMC 3708 • Explorers of North America • ©2003 by Evan-Moor Corp.

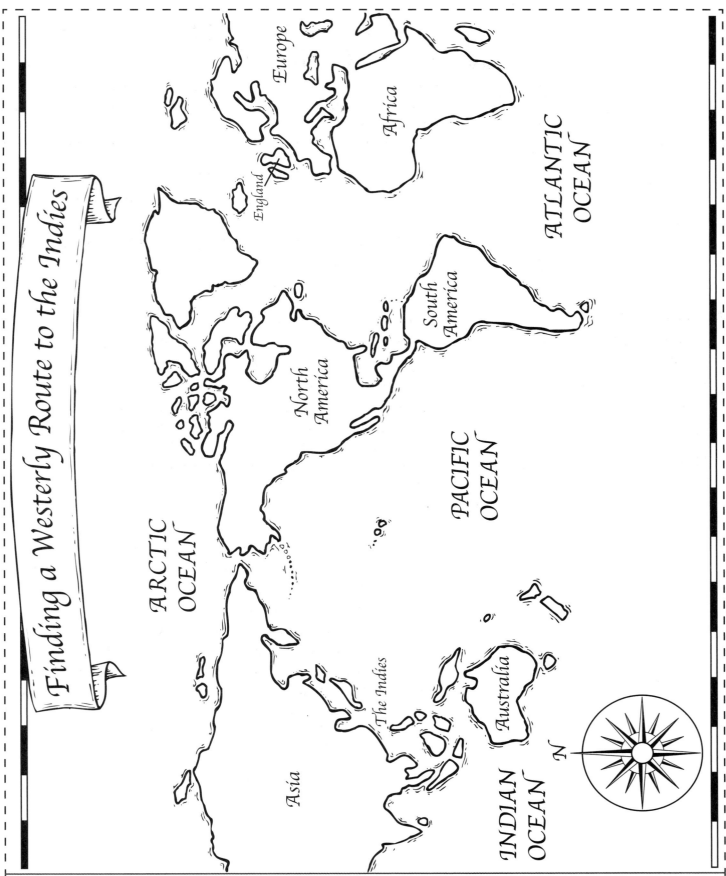

Finding a Westerly Route to the Indies

Europe

Africa

England

ATLANTIC
OCEAN

South
America

North
America

ARCTIC
OCEAN

PACIFIC
OCEAN

Asia

The Indies

Australia

INDIAN
OCEAN

N

Cut out map. Roll map back.
Tuck this tab under, and paper–clip at top and bottom edges to hold map in a cylinder shape.

Pocket 4

HERNANDO CORTES

FAST FACTS

Hernando Cortes . . . . **page 29**
See page 2 for information on how to prepare the Fast Facts bookmark and pocket label. Use the bookmark for a quick review during transition times throughout the day.

ABOUT

Hernando Cortes . . . . **page 30**
Reproduce this page for students. Read and discuss the background information about Hernando Cortes, highlighting important information to remember. Incorporate library and multimedia resources that are available.

ACTIVITIES

Map of Cortes's Route . . . . **page 31**
Reproduce this page for students. Have students color Cortes's exploration route. Glue the map onto 9" x 12" (23 x 30.5 cm) construction paper. Place the completed map in the pocket.

A Long Sea Voyage . . . . **pages 32–34**
Sailors stored all their belongings in a sea chest. Students make a sea chest and write about what they would take on a voyage with Cortes.

A Peaceful Story About Cortes . . . . . . **pages 35 & 36**
Students decide on their own peaceful endings for Cortes's expedition to Mexico. They write them as brief announcements, which they read to the class.

EMC 3708 • Explorers of North America • ©2003 by Evan-Moor Corp.

HERNANDO CORTES

HERNANDO CORTES

FAST FACTS

- Cortes, along with 600 men, 20 horses, and 10 small cannons, conquered the Aztec empire of 5 million people.

- The Aztecs were at first terrified of the pale faces and hairy skin of Cortes and his men. They thought the strangers rode monsters (horses) and carried sticks that roared like thunder (guns).

- Cortes and his men wore suits of armor that included a helmet and breastplate. They carried battle-axes and swords.

- Cortes and his men were horrified to find that the Aztecs sacrificed humans to their gods.

- It took Cortes two years to conquer Mexico.

- In 1536 Cortes led an expedition that discovered Baja California.

- Cortes retired from a soldier's life in 1541. He lived in luxury in Spain until his death in 1547.

ABOUT
HERNANDO CORTES

During the 1500s, a Spanish ruler named Diego Velasquez heard stories about a huge and wealthy Aztec empire in Mexico.

He wanted to conquer the Aztecs and get their gold. He chose Hernando Cortes to lead the expedition.

In 1519 Cortes set sail from the southern coast of Cuba. He had 11 ships, 600 sailors, and horses with him. They sailed west through the Gulf of Mexico and landed on the eastern coast of Mexico. There, friendly Indians gave Cortes gifts, including gold.

These Indians sent a message about Cortes's arrival to the Aztec ruler, Montezuma. Montezuma was 200 miles away in the Aztec capital city of Tenochtitlan. Montezuma believed that one day a great white god would appear from the ocean to the east. Montezuma wondered if Cortes was the great white god. Montezuma sent gifts of gold to Cortes and asked him to leave. When Cortes saw the gold, though, he wanted more.

Cortes made plans to go to the Aztec capital. First, he and his crew started building a fort in a town they named Vera Cruz. To keep his soldiers from abandoning him, Cortes had most of his ships burned. He loaded one ship with Montezuma's gold and sent it back to Spain. Cortes set off with his soldiers and a few hundred Cempaolan Indians, who didn't like the Aztecs, to capture the capital.

Finally, Cortes and his growing army reached Tenochtitlan. It was a beautiful city. Montezuma greeted Cortes at his palace. While there, Cortes's men discovered that the palace had a secret room filled with treasures. The Aztecs became worried that the explorers would take their gold. Montezuma also realized that Cortes was just a man. A bloody battle broke out. In the end, Cortes and his army won the battle and conquered the Aztecs. Cortes also got what he came after—gold.

Cortes renamed the capital Mexico City. They also renamed the country New Spain, and Cortes was appointed governor. The Spanish spread their Christian religion to the native tribes. By 1524 New Spain had become the richest and largest area owned by Spain. Spain was now the most powerful nation in Europe.

 EMC 3708 • Explorers of North America •©2003 by Evan-Moor Corp.

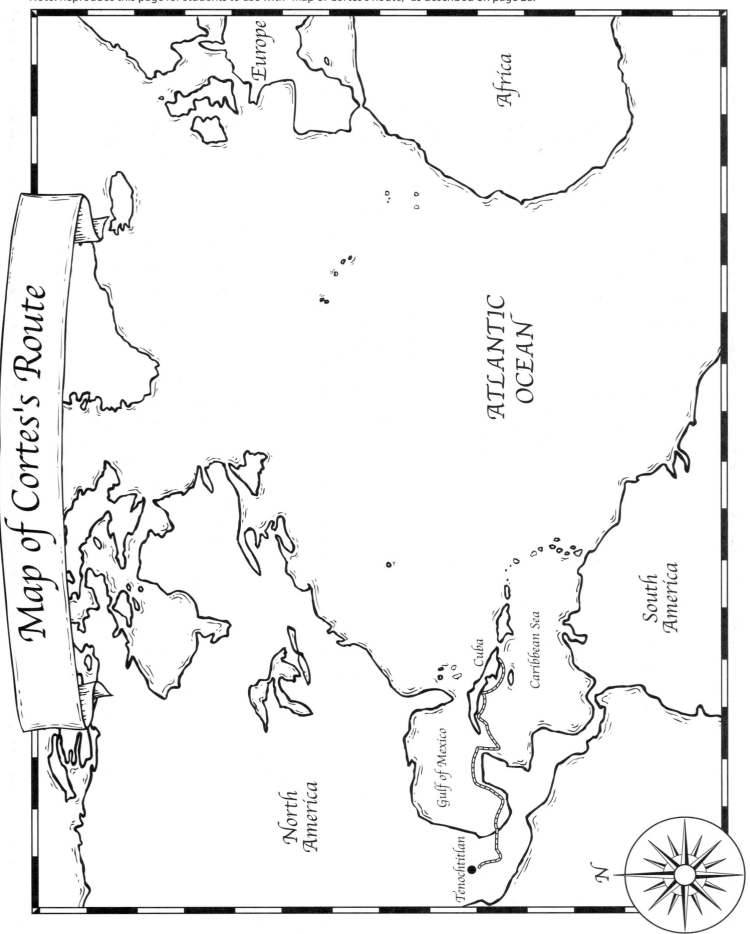

Map of Cortes's Route

Europe

Africa

ATLANTIC OCEAN

North America

Gulf of Mexico

Cuba

Caribbean Sea

South America

Tenochtitlan

N

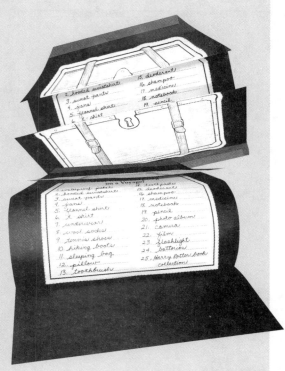

A LONG SEA VOYAGE

Students make a double-hinged sea chest and "fill" it with important personal possessions for a voyage with Cortes.

STEPS TO FOLLOW

Guide students through the following steps to "fill" their sea chest:

1. Explain that there wasn't much space for personal belongings on sailing ships of the 1500s. Everything a crewman needed had to fit in his sea chest.

2. Students pretend they are going on Cortes's expedition to Mexico. They may take 25 modern-day items with them for the two-year voyage. Cortes will supply the food and weapons, but they will each need at least 10 items of clothing and 15 other items. Brainstorm as a class about what modern-day clothes and small items they would pack. Have them explain why they chose those items.

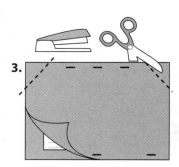

3. On the writing form, students number to 25 and list their chosen personal belongings.

Guide students through the following steps to make the sea chest:

1. Staple the writing form to one sheet of black paper. Trim the corners.

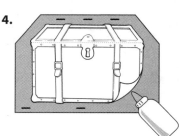

2. Lay the other sheet of black paper on top and trim the corners to match.

3. Staple the top and bottom edges.

4. Color and cut out the trunk pattern. Glue it to the top sheet of black paper.

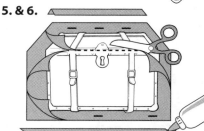

5. Cut the trunk along the cut line through the pattern and the top sheet of black paper only.

6. Fold and glue the binding strips over the stapled edges.

MATERIALS

- trunk pattern on page 33, reproduced for each student
- writing form on page 34, reproduced for each student
- two 9" x 12" (23 x 30.5 cm) sheets of black construction paper
- 1" x 9" (2.5 x 23 cm) and 1" x 12" (2.5 x 30.5 cm) strips of paper for binding
- stapler
- marking pens, colored pencils, or crayons
- glue

DESIGN A SEA CHEST

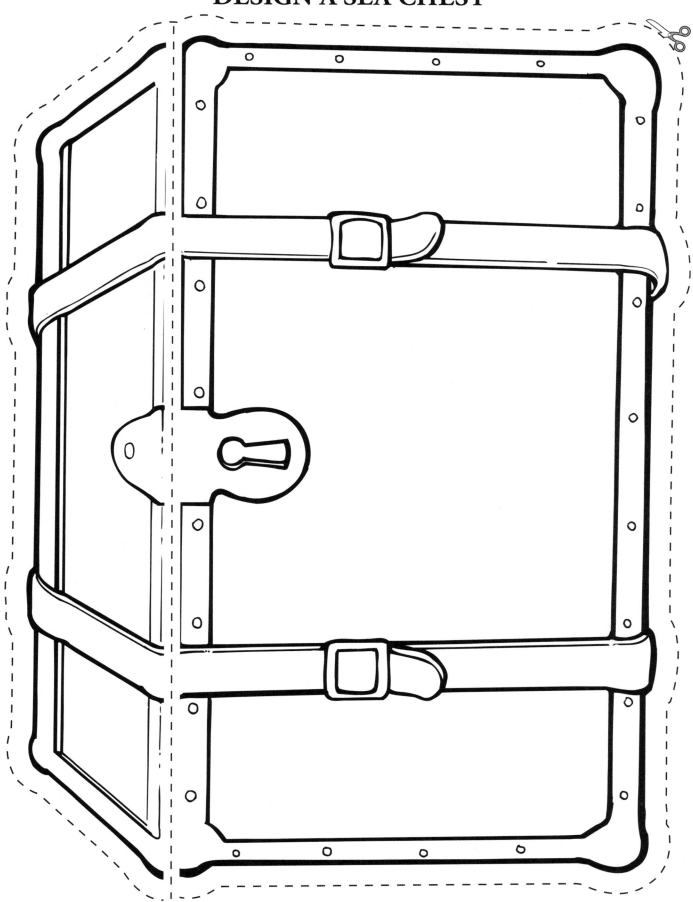

DESIGN A SEA CHEST

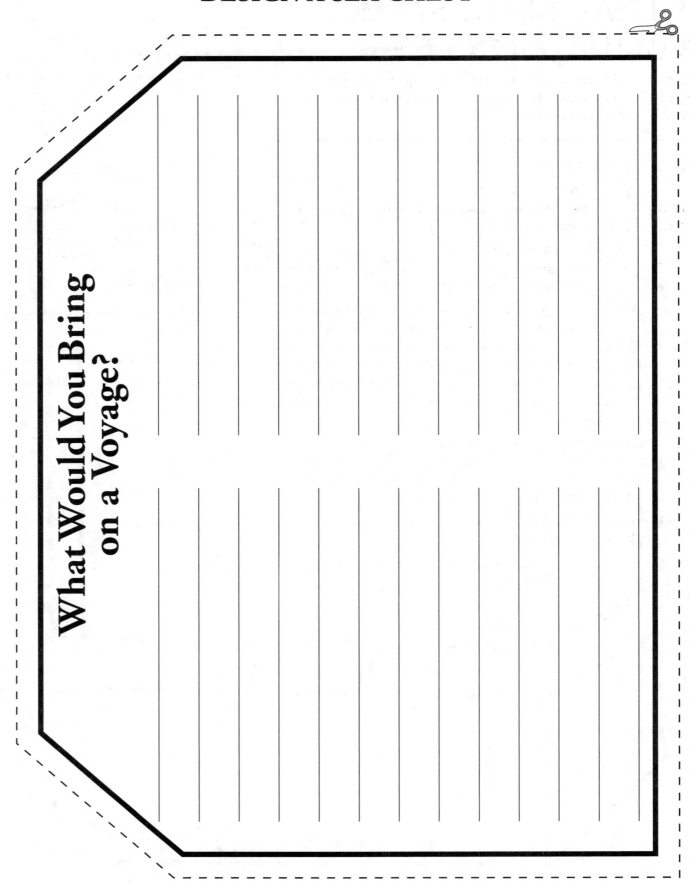

What Would You Bring on a Voyage?

A PEACEFUL STORY ABOUT CORTES

Students decide on their own peaceful endings for Cortes's expedition to Mexico. They write them as brief announcements, which they read to the class.

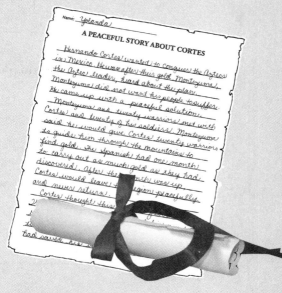

STEPS TO FOLLOW

1. Review the information about Cortes from the "About Hernando Cortes" sheet with students. Have them retell the story of Cortes's victory over the Aztecs.

2. Talk about what the Aztecs lost when they were conquered by Cortes. (Possible answers: their land, buildings on the land, gold, what the gold could buy, and the people killed in battle.)

3. Brainstorm with the class on more peaceful ways that Cortes might have gotten gold and land. (Possible answers: He could have purchased the land and gold from the Aztecs or traded things for the gold and land. The Spanish could have worked for the Aztecs in exchange for the gold and land. He could have asked the Aztecs to help them search for their own land and gold somewhere else.)

4. Tell students they get to decide on their own peaceful endings for Cortes's expedition. Have students write their peaceful stories about Cortes as brief announcements on the scroll pattern from page 36.

5. Then instruct them to roll the paper up and tie it with yarn or ribbon like a scroll.

6. The students take turns unrolling their scrolls and making their "announcements" to the class.

MATERIALS

- page 36, reproduced for each student
- pencil or pen
- 24" (61 cm) yarn or ribbon

Name: _____

A PEACEFUL STORY ABOUT CORTES

_____

_____

_____

_____

_____

_____

_____

_____

_____

_____

_____

_____

_____

_____

_____

_____

_____

_____

JACQUES CARTIER

FAST FACTS

See page 2 for information on how to prepare the Fast Facts bookmark and pocket label. Use the bookmark for a quick review during transition times throughout the day.

ABOUT

Reproduce this page for students. Read and discuss the background information about Jacques Cartier, highlighting important information to remember. Incorporate library and multimedia resources that are available.

ACTIVITIES

Reproduce this page for students. Have students color Cartier's exploration routes. Glue the map onto 9" x 12" (23 x 30.5 cm) construction paper. Place the completed map in the pocket.

Sea captains kept a ship's log on their expeditions. Students pretend they are sea captains and design the cover of their own ship's log. Then the "captains" write two entries into their logs.

Students design a game board, based on their knowledge of Cartier's voyages.

JACQUES CARTIER

JACQUES CARTIER

FAST FACTS

- It took Cartier and his crew 20 days to cross the Atlantic.

- Cartier discovered that Newfoundland was an island, not a peninsula as was previously thought.

- Friendly Indians acted as guides for Cartier's explorations.

- The Indians showed the French how to cure scurvy with a tea made from bark and needles of the white cedar tree.

- The Indian name for the St. Lawrence River means "The River That Walks."

- The Hurons told stories about a land in the north full of gold and other treasure. This was not true, but the French liked stories of riches and the Hurons liked telling stories.

- The Huron chief let two of his sons sail to France with Cartier.

- Cartier took large quantities of pyrite and quartz back to France, thinking they were gold and diamonds.

- Cartier's men also brought back corn. This was probably the first corn ever seen in northern Europe.

- Cartier died on his estate in France at the age of 66.

ABOUT
JACQUES CARTIER

In the early 1500s, France decided to find a short route to the Indies by trying a northern route around America. This route was called the Northwest Passage.

In 1534 a Frenchman named Jacques Cartier set off from St. Malo, France, to find the passage. He had two ships and a crew of 62 men. Cartier headed northwest. He reached Newfoundland and sailed around its northern tip to Labrador. On land, he set up a cross and claimed the area for France. He named the land New France.

After leaving Labrador, Cartier sailed southwest and discovered a gulf. The gulf was later named the Gulf of St. Lawrence. Cartier explored lands around the gulf. He bought furs from the native tribes, who told Cartier their country was named Canada.

Cartier kept looking for the Northwest Passage. Finally, he discovered a river flowing west from the gulf. He thought it might lead to the Pacific Ocean. But it was late summer, and the weather would soon become cold. With no time left to explore this river, Cartier headed back to France.

In July of 1535, the King of France sent Cartier back to explore the river. This time, Cartier had three ships and a crew of 100 men. He finally reached the river, which was later named the St. Lawrence River. As he sailed west along the St. Lawrence, the water became shallow. He had to leave behind his largest ships and set off in small boats. Cartier ended up in an area that is now called Montreal. There, he met a tribe of friendly Huron Indians.

The French explorers turned back when they didn't find a Northwest Passage. They traveled the river back to where they had left their ships. Men who had stayed behind with the ships had built a fort. In this area, later named Quebec, Cartier and his crew spent a very cold winter. Many men became ill with scurvy. The Indians taught Cartier and his crew how to cure scurvy, so his men were saved. When the weather warmed, Cartier and his men sailed back to France.

A new French king gave Cartier money to sail back and set up a colony in the new country. The colony failed, mostly because of the freezing weather of Canada's winters.

During the next 20 years, France was at war and lost interest in Canada and finding a Northwest Passage.

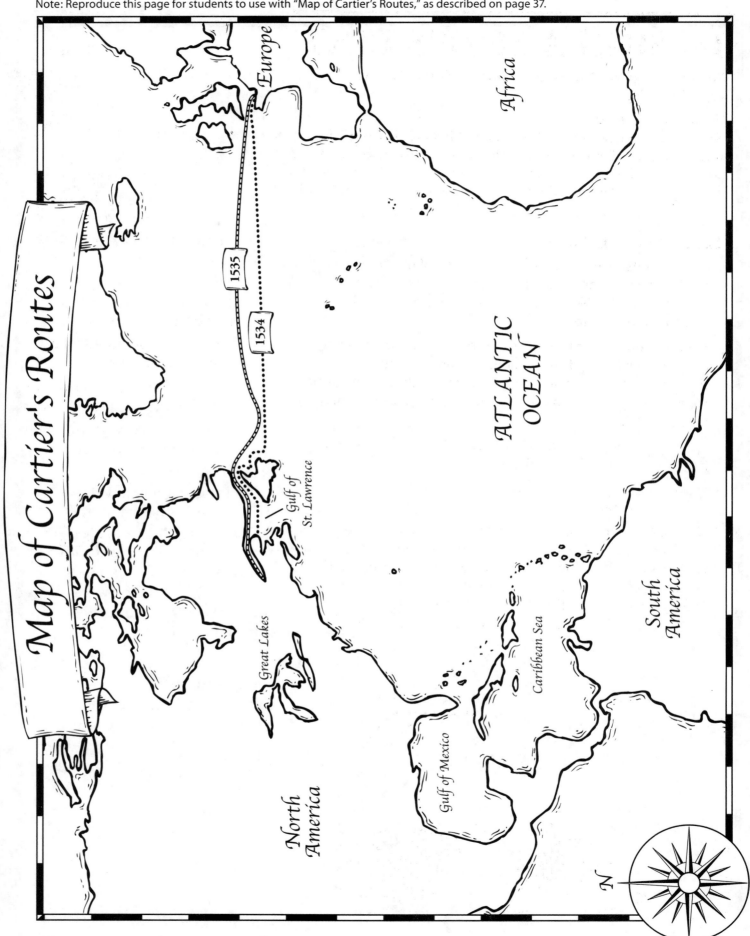

Map of Cartier's Routes

Europe

Africa

1535

1534

ATLANTIC OCEAN

Gulf of St. Lawrence

Great Lakes

Caribbean Sea

South America

North America

Gulf of Mexico

N

DESIGN A SHIP'S LOG

Students design the cover of their own ship's log. Then they write pages in the log.

Share with Students

Sea captains like Jacques Cartier kept a ship's log. The ship's log was like a journal of the trip. It included dates, distances traveled, landmarks sighted, and what the weather was like. The captain also included personal observations of problems that occurred onboard.

STEPS TO FOLLOW

1. Ask students to imagine they are captains of their own ships during the 1500s and, like Cartier, they have been asked by France to find the Northwest Passage. Have them think of a name for their ships.

2. Have students make the ship's log cover out of construction paper. Students include their name, written as "Captain _____," the name of their ship, and a drawing of the ship on the front cover (or you may reproduce the small ship picture on this page for students).

3. Instruct students to cut the log pages. Then they staple the log pages inside a front and back cover.

4. Have students punch two holes at the top of the construction paper log and tie ribbon through the holes.

5. Ask your student "captains" to fill out their logs, making notes and drawing pictures of what they would see and do during four days of their journey. Ideas for the entries might include such things as compass directions, maps, sea animals spotted, condition of the sailors, and supply lists.

MATERIALS

- page 41, reproduced for each student (optional)
- page 42, reproduced twice for each student
- two 6" x 9" (15 x 23 cm) pieces of construction paper
- crayons, marking pens, or colored pencils
- scissors
- two 15" (38 cm) pieces of ribbon or yarn
- hole punch
- stapler

DESIGN A SHIP'S LOG

EMC 3708 • Explorers of North America •©2003 by Evan-Moor Corp.

CARTIER'S JOURNEY GAME BOARD

Students create game boards based on Cartier's voyage in 1535.

STEPS TO FOLLOW

1. On the chalkboard, draw a two-column chart. Label the left column "Good Things" and the right column "Bad Things."

2. Discuss Cartier's second voyage to Canada, in 1535, from the "About Jacques Cartier" information page. During your discussion, fill in the chart with brief descriptions of the good and bad things that happened during that voyage.

   For example, good things might be that he had more ships and a larger crew; he made it back to the St. Lawrence River; they met friendly Indians; the Indians taught Cartier how to cure scurvy by drinking tea made from white cedar trees.

   Bad things might be that they had to leave ships and boats behind as they sailed farther up the St. Lawrence River and it got shallower; they didn't find the Northwest Passage; they spent a cold winter; Cartier's men became ill with scurvy.

3. Hand out copies of page 45 to students. Students write four "good things" about Cartier's 1535 voyage in random squares on their game boards. Have students lightly color over those squares in a color of their choice.

4. Students write four "bad things" in random squares on their game boards. Have students lightly color over those squares in another color.

5. For the rest of the squares students draw a small picture of a ship, compass, or any item associated with the explorer.

6. Instruct students to glue the paper game to a piece of tagboard to make it sturdier.

7. Hand out the spinner pattern and rules for the game on page 44. Have students make their own spinner following the directions given on the page.

8. Direct students to also cut out the rules for the game. Go over the rules and then have students take turns playing the game together.

9. Optional: You may give the students a blank game board and have them make up their own game and rules to go with it.

MATERIALS

- pages 44 and 45, reproduced for each student
- tagboard
- pencil
- scissors
- glue
- paper fastener
- game pieces: plastic disks of various colors, or other similar items

CARTIER'S JOURNEY GAME

The object of the game is to be the first to return home to "France," which is the last square. Two to four people may play.

DIRECTIONS

1. Place the game pieces on the starting square, which is "France."

2. Players take turns spinning the spinner to see how many spaces to move at a time.

3. If the player lands on a square with a "good" thing about Cartier's journey noted on it, the player gets to move two more spaces ahead and stay there until the next turn.

4. If the player lands on a square with a "bad" thing about Cartier's journey noted on it, the player has to go back one space and stay there until the next turn.

5. If the player lands on a picture space, the player waits until the next turn.

6. If more than one player lands on the same space, they share the space until the next turn.

7. The player who makes it to "End France" first is the winner.

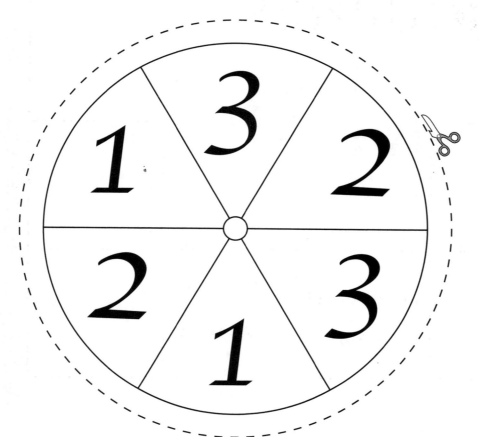

SPINNER ASSEMBLY

Glue the spinner patterns to a piece of tagboard and cut them out. Poke a hole through both pieces where shown. Fasten the two parts together with a paper fastener.

   EMC 3708 • Explorers of North America •©2003 by Evan-Moor Corp.

CARTIER'S JOURNEY GAME BOARD

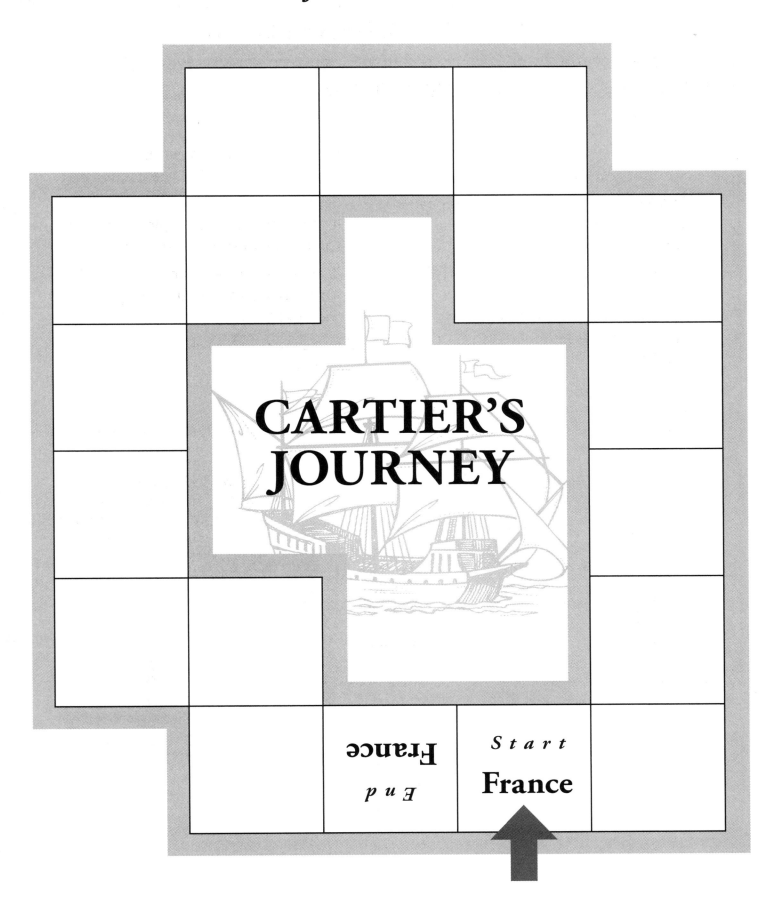

CARTIER'S JOURNEY

End France

Start France

SIR FRANCIS DRAKE

FAST FACTS

Sir Francis Drake . . . . **page 47**
See page 2 for information on how to prepare the Fast Facts bookmark and pocket label. Use the bookmark for a quick review during transition times throughout the day.

ABOUT

Sir Francis Drake . . . . **page 48**
Reproduce this page for students. Read and discuss the background information about Sir Francis Drake, highlighting important information to remember. Incorporate library and multimedia resources that are available.

ACTIVITIES

Map of Drake's Route . . . . **page 49**
Reproduce this page for students. Have students color Drake's exploration route. Glue the map onto 9" x 12" (23 x 30.5 cm) construction paper. Place the completed map in the pocket.

Design an Old Ship . . . . **pages 50 & 51**
The two kinds of ships used by explorers were the caravel and the carrack. Students look at pictures of two old ships. Students then design their own sailing vessel.

Weather Reports from Cape Horn . . . **pages 52 & 53**
Students report the weather Drake encountered as he traveled around the tip of South America.

SIR FRANCIS DRAKE

SIR FRANCIS DRAKE

FAST FACTS

- Drake went to sea at the age of 12 or 13 as an apprentice on a small trading ship. When he died, the ship's owner left the ship to Drake.

- It took Drake three years, from 1577 to 1580, to sail around the world.

- Queen Elizabeth I of England knighted Drake. He was then known as Sir Francis Drake.

- To the English, Drake was a hero. The Spanish saw him as a pirate.

- Drake was brave and sometimes heartless in battle. He was kind to his crew, but demanded loyalty and respect from them.

- Drake, as commander of a large group of warships, played an important part in the defeat of the Spanish Armada in 1588.

- Drake died at sea in 1596. His body was placed inside a lead casket and slipped overboard.

ABOUT
SIR FRANCIS DRAKE

Francis Drake was born in Devon, England, in the 1540s. As a young boy, he worked on English ships.

In 1577 England's Queen Elizabeth sent Drake on a secret voyage to America. She wanted him to make surprise attacks on Spanish ships and lands in the new continent. England didn't like that Spain controlled much of the New World.

In November of 1577, Drake set sail with five ships and 150 men. He headed toward the Strait of Magellan, a narrow 350-mile-long (563 km) waterway at the southern end of South America. When Drake reached this area, there was a storm. He thought his two smallest ships wouldn't make it through. He took the crews of these two ships onto the other three larger ships. The two little ships were burned. The remaining three ships sailed onward. The storm became violent. One ship sank, and the other sailed back to England. Only Drake's ship, the *Golden Hind,* made it through the Strait of Magellan.

Drake turned his ship north and sailed up the western side of South America. Midway up present-day Chile, Drake came upon a Spanish town called Valpariso. There, he raided a Spanish ship and stole gold, silver, and jewels. Drake continued sailing north, raiding Spanish towns and ships as he went. He was so quick that the Spanish couldn't warn the next settlements in time.

Drake and his crew continued sailing north. They ended up just north of San Francisco Bay, along California's coast. There, the English met friendly Indians and traded with them. Drake claimed this land for England and called it New Albion. Today, this area is known as Drake's Bay.

In July 1579, Drake headed back to England. He didn't want to take the southern route back by the Spanish settlements and risk being attacked. Instead, he took a western route across the Pacific Ocean. After sailing around the southern tip of Africa, he reached England in September of 1580. He was the first Englishman to have sailed around the world.

 EMC 3708 • Explorers of North America • ©2003 by Evan-Moor Corp.

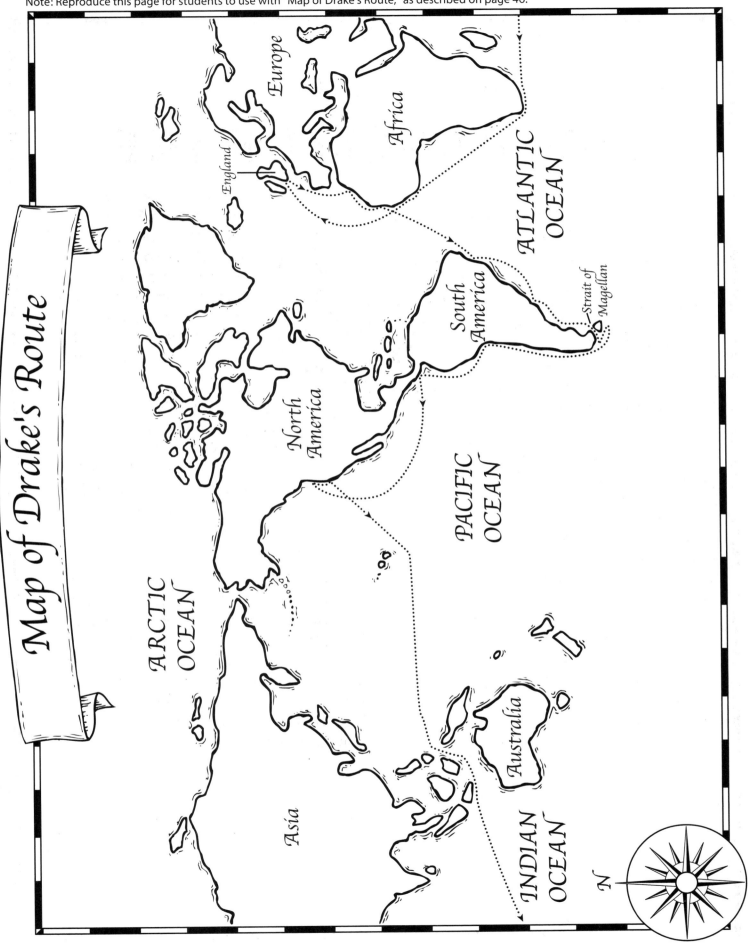

Map of Drake's Route

Europe

England

Africa

ATLANTIC OCEAN

Strait of Magellan

South America

North America

PACIFIC OCEAN

ARCTIC OCEAN

Asia

Australia

INDIAN OCEAN

N

MATERIALS

- page 51, reproduced for each student
- scratch paper
- 9" x 12" (23 x 30.5 cm) white construction paper
- pencil
- crayons or colored pencils

DESIGN AN OLD SHIP

Students look at pictures of two old sailing ships and then design their own ships.

STEPS TO FOLLOW

1. Hand out copies of page 51. Ask students to study the pictures of the two types of ships and read the information about them. Ask how the ships are alike. (Both have several sails. They have long wooden hulls, and their fronts rise to a point. Their rear decks are high.) Ask how the ships are different. (One is called a caravel, the other a carrack. One has triangular sails, the other has a triangular sail and several square sails. One has one sail per mast, the other has several sails per mast.) Talk about the parts of the ships.

2. Tell students that they get to be ship designers in England in the 1500s. They should use designs similar to the caravel and carrack. Students will need to decide if the ship should be smaller like the caravel, larger like the carrack, or a combination of the two.

3. Have them sketch out ideas on scratch paper before drawing and coloring their final designs on the white construction paper.

4. Direct students to give their new ship a special name.

EMC 3708 • Explorers of North America •©2003 by Evan-Moor Corp.

DESIGN AN OLD SHIP

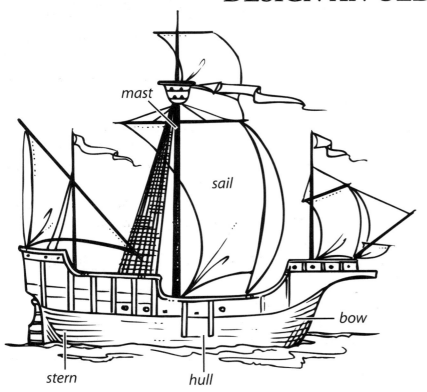

CARRACK

The carrack was developed after the caravel. It was designed to carry large crews and cargo on long ocean trips, so it was much larger and slower than the caravel. The carrack often had some lateen sails, but most of its sails were square-rigged sails. These sails were attached to horizontal poles on the ships' masts. The square-rigged sail was used to catch wind from behind. Columbus's main ship, the *Santa Maria*, was a carrack. So was Drake's ship, the *Golden Hind.*

CARAVEL

The caravel was a small, light, and speedy ship. The caravel usually had triangular sails called lateen sails. These sails were attached to sloping poles on the ship's masts. Sailors could change the angle of the lateen sails so the ship could sail in any direction. Europeans probably learned about the lateen sails from Arab traders. Europeans developed the caravel in the 1400s. Columbus's ships, the *Nina* and the *Pinta,* were caravels.

WEATHER REPORTS FROM CAPE HORN

Students report on the bad weather that befell Sir Francis Drake as he rounded Cape Horn.

MATERIALS

- large world map
- information on the bottom of this page, reproduced for each student
- page 53, reproduced for each student
- 6" x 18" (15 x 45.5 cm) construction paper
- scissors
- glue
- pencil
- optional: crayons or colored pencils

STEPS TO FOLLOW

1. Use a large world map to show students the southern tip of South America. Read "Bad Weather Ahead" to learn about weather in this region. Reread the "About Sir Francis Drake" information sheet to recall Drake's struggles while sailing through the Strait of Magellan.

2. Instruct students to refer to the information presented to create weather reports during Drake's passage through the Strait of Magellan. The heading on each writing form tells Drake's location.

3. To create a folder to hold the weather report, students accordion-fold the construction paper as shown.

4. Cut out the weather report cover, the "Bad Weather Ahead" information sheet, and the three written reports and glue them into the folder as shown in the photograph.

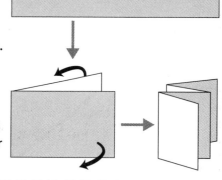

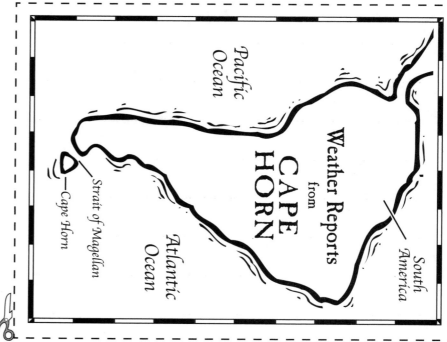

WEATHER REPORTS FROM CAPE HORN

Bad Weather Ahead

Sir Francis Drake had to sail through the Strait of Magellan at the southern tip of South America. The point of land below the Strait of Magellan is called Cape Horn.

The weather around Cape Horn is stormy, and many ships were destroyed in this area. There are no landmasses to block the westerly winds. The unblocked winds bring severe storms. Furthermore, the Andes Mountains, which run down the western coast of South America, force wind and storms south toward Cape Horn.

Drake had to make sure he sailed through the Strait of Magellan during the summer, when the weather was best. Summers are short near the South Pole, so Drake had only a brief period of time.

Approaching the Strait of Magellan

_____

_____

_____

_____

_____

_____

_____

Sailing Through the Strait

_____

_____

_____

_____

_____

_____

_____

Reaching the Pacific Ocean

_____

_____

_____

_____

_____

_____

_____

Pocket 7

HENRY HUDSON

FAST FACTS

See page 2 for information on how to prepare the Fast
Facts bookmark and pocket label. Use the bookmark
for a quick review during transition times throughout
the day.

ABOUT

Reproduce this page for students. Read and discuss
the background information about Henry Hudson,
highlighting important information to remember.
Incorporate library and multimedia resources that are
available.

ACTIVITIES

Reproduce this page for students. Have students
color Hudson's exploration routes. Glue the map onto
9" x 12" (23 x 30.5 cm) construction paper. Place the
completed map in the pocket.

Navigators on explorers' ships used two important
tools—parallel rulers and dividers. Students pretend
they are navigators when they make and use parallel
rulers and dividers.

Students write a newspaper account of what they
think might have happened to Hudson when his
crew abandoned him.

HENRY HUDSON

HENRY HUDSON

FAST FACTS

- Henry Hudson's date of birth is unknown. Date estimates range from 1550 to 1575—quite a difference!

- Hudson had three sons. His son John sailed on all four of Hudson's voyages.

- Hudson sailed as far south as present-day North Carolina. He also explored Chesapeake Bay and Delaware Bay.

- When the *Discovery* survivors reached England, they were imprisoned.

- Hudson's wife, Katherine, persuaded the Dutch East India Company to send a rescue ship to find her husband and son. The ship never found a trace of the men.

- Katherine sought compensation from the Dutch East India Company for the loss of her husband and son. Company records called her "that troublesome and impatient woman."

- Katherine tried unsuccessfully to have a monument erected to honor Hudson.

ABOUT
HENRY HUDSON

By the 1600s, Europeans had found southern routes to the Indies. However, they had not found a northern route.

In 1602 the Dutch started a trading business called the Dutch East India Company. One of their goals was to search for a Northwest Passage to the Indies. The company found an experienced sailor named Henry Hudson to lead the search.

In 1609 Hudson set off from the Netherlands with a crew of 20. They sailed in a ship called the *Half Moon*. As they traveled north, the weather grew colder and colder. Hudson abandoned his search for the Northwest Passage, turned the ship around, and sailed southwest toward America.

The *Half Moon* sailed past Newfoundland and down the eastern coast of America. Where New York is today, Hudson found a harbor and a river that flowed into it. Thinking the river might be the Northwest Passage to the Pacific Ocean, Hudson sailed up it. When the river became too shallow, he realized it was not the passage. He turned the *Half Moon* around. While he sailed along this river, Hudson traded metal for furs from local Indian tribes. The Dutch soon set up trading posts along this river, which was later named the Hudson River.

In 1610 England hired Hudson to find the Northwest Passage. Hudson sailed off to northern Canada in a ship called the *Discovery*. He was sure he had found the Northwest Passage when he discovered a 450-mile-long passageway. The passageway, later called Hudson Strait, led to a large bay, now called Hudson Bay. Hudson kept searching the shores of the bay for a water route to the Pacific Ocean. When winter set in, the bay froze over. The *Discovery* froze in the ice. Hudson and his crew spent a hard winter in a log hut.

In June of 1611, when the weather warmed, Hudson set sail. The crew thought Hudson was sailing back home to England, but they soon realized he was sailing west to continue searching for the Northwest Passage. Wanting desperately to go home, the angry crew put Hudson, his son, and seven other loyal crewmen into a small boat with no oars, and left them in the bay. Hudson and the others in the boat were never heard from again.

   EMC 3708 • Explorers of North America •©2003 by Evan-Moor Corp.

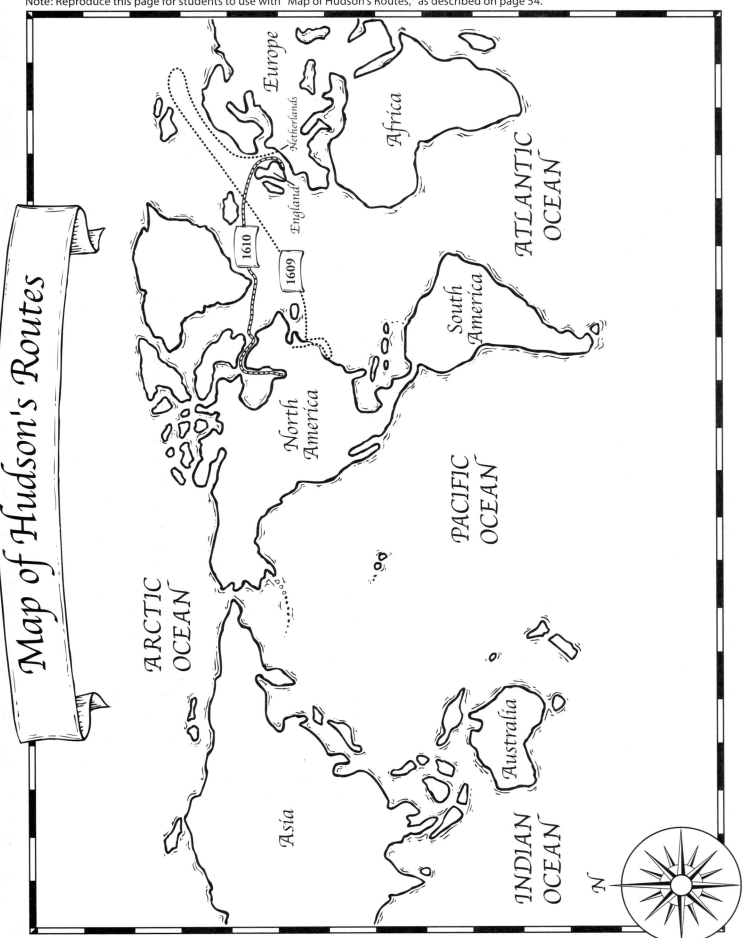

Map of Hudson's Routes

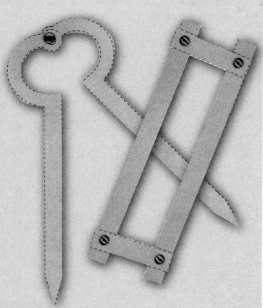

MATERIALS

- pages 59 and 60, reproduced for each student or group of students
- tagboard or manila file folders
- pencil
- scissors
- hole punch
- ½" (1.25 cm) paper fasteners, five per student

NAVIGATIONAL TOOLS

Students make their own parallel rulers and dividers. Then they practice using the instruments just like real cartographers.

Share with Students

Navigators on ships used several tools to help them plan routes. Two of the tools were parallel rulers and dividers. Parallel rulers were used with a chart to determine the course along a given compass bearing. Parallel rulers were used to draw a line that was parallel to a given line. Dividers were used to measure the distance between two given points.

STEPS TO FOLLOW

1. Make a parallel ruler and dividers to show students before they begin the project. Discuss their uses to mapmakers and demonstrate using a large map.

2. Have students glue the parallel ruler and divider pieces onto tagboard. Allow to dry.

3. Direct students to then cut out the ruler and divider pieces.

4. Assemble as shown.

5. Have students use the parallel ruler and dividers following the directions on page 60.

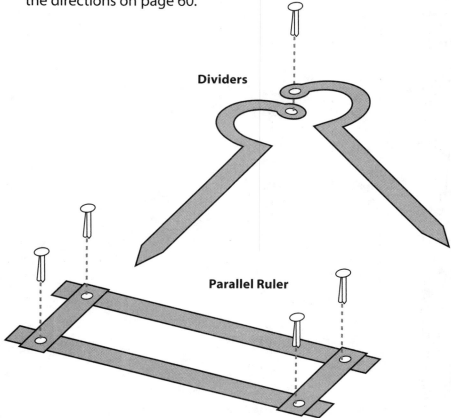

Dividers

Parallel Ruler

MAPMAKING TOOLS

Parallel Ruler   **Dividers**

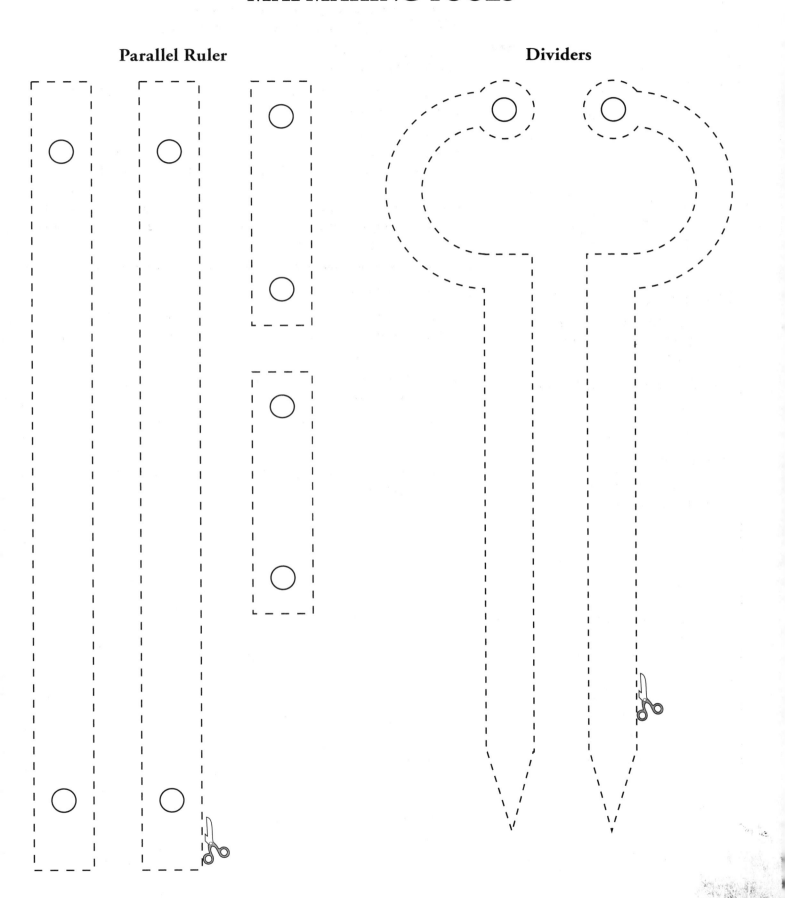

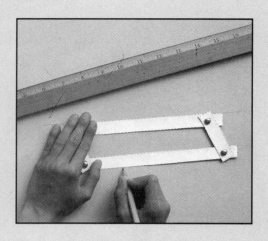

MATERIALS

- parallel ruler and dividers
- unlined paper
- pencil
- ruler

HOW TO USE THE PARALLEL RULER AND DIVIDERS

Now that you have made the parallel ruler and dividers, you get a chance to practice using them.

Parallel Ruler

STEPS TO FOLLOW

1. Draw a straight line with a standard ruler.

2. Hold the two shorter sides of the parallel ruler, and straighten them out until they are perpendicular to the two longer sides and the parallel ruler is a rectangle.

3. Line up one long edge of the parallel ruler with the line already drawn with the ruler.

4. Holding the parallel ruler in the rectangle shape, draw a second line along the opposite long edge of the parallel ruler. The second line should be parallel to the original line drawn with the ruler.

5. Adjust the slant of the two shorter sides—making the parallel ruler into a parallelogram shape—and draw several lines of varying distances to the original ruler-drawn line.

Dividers

STEPS TO FOLLOW

1. Draw two dots on unlined paper.

2. Put one point of the dividers on one dot. Then slide the legs of the divider apart until the other point sits on the other dot.

3. Keeping the dividers opened to the same distance, move them to another place on the paper. Put one divider point on the paper and draw a new dot under that point.

4. Then set the other point down on the paper and draw a dot under it. The second set of dots should be the same distance apart as the first set of dots.

EMC 3708 • Explorers of North America •©2003 by Evan-Moor Corp.

WHAT HAPPENED TO HUDSON?

Students write a newspaper account of what they think might have happened to Hudson when his crew abandoned him.

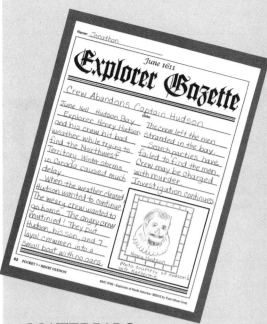

STEPS TO FOLLOW

1. Recall that on Hudson's second voyage, his crew pulled Hudson, his son, and seven other people from the ship and left them behind in a small boat without oars. They were never heard from again. Tell your students they get to come up with their own stories about what happened to Hudson and the others after they were abandoned. Students write their stories as newspaper articles in an imaginary 1600s newspaper called the *Explorer Gazette*.

2. Write the following on the chalkboard: Who? When? Where? What? Why? How? Explain that newspaper articles usually answer these six questions about an event. Who was involved? When did it happen? Where did it happen? What happened? Why did the event happen? How did it happen?

3. Ask your students what they would write for their stories as an answer to "Who?" (Hudson, his son, and the crew left behind in the small boat). Ask what they would write for "When?" (June 1611). Tell students that the answers to the three remaining questions are up to them.

4. Ask students to write these same six words down the left side of their writing paper, leaving room between each word. Based on their own stories about what happened to Hudson, students answer each question.

5. Students use the answers to the six questions to help them write newspaper articles in paragraph form. Their articles should include an introduction, body, and conclusion.

6. Hand out copies of page 62 to each student. Students write their front-page stories on the lines provided. They should also include a story title, as well as a picture.

7. Invite students to share their newspaper stories with the class.

MATERIALS

- page 62, reproduced for each student
- pencil or pen
- writing paper
- crayons or marking pens

Name: _____

Explorer Gazette

(title)

_____

_____   _____

_____   _____

_____   _____

_____   _____

_____   _____

_____   _____

_____

_____

_____

_____

_____

_____

_____

_____

Pocket 8

DANIEL BOONE

FAST FACTS

See page 2 for information on how to prepare the Fast Facts bookmark and pocket label. Use the bookmark for a quick review during transition times throughout the day.

ABOUT

Reproduce this page for students. Read and discuss the background information about Daniel Boone, highlighting important information to remember. Incorporate library and multimedia resources that are available.

ACTIVITIES

Reproduce this page for students. Have students locate and color Boone's exploration route on the map. Glue the map onto 9" x 12" (23 x 30.5 cm) construction paper. Place the completed map in the pocket.

Daniel Boone's life was so exciting and poetic. Students write a limerick about this famous explorer.

Students write a legend based on an actual event from Daniel Boone's life. Provide writing paper and large construction paper on which to mount the stories.

DANIEL BOONE

FAST FACTS

- Daniel did not go to school. A relative taught him to read when he was older.

- Both his brother and son were killed during raids on the Shawnee.

- Boone served in the Virginia Assembly in 1781. He was captured by invading British troops, but was soon released.

- The only original portrait of Daniel Boone was painted by Mr. Chester Harding in 1820. It now hangs in the State House in Frankfort, Kentucky.

- Daniel's career as a huntsman began at age 12, when his father gave him a rifle.

- Daniel Boone was captured four times by Indians. One time, his companion, Stewart, was killed. Boone always escaped.

- Daniel Boone's role as a wilderness scout was the inspiration for the organization of the Boy Scouts of America in the early 1900s.

- Boone took his last hunting trip at the age of 83.

ABOUT
DANIEL BOONE

Daniel Boone's family moved from England to Pennsylvania in 1712. The family later moved to North Carolina, and Boone's young life was full of hunting and trapping.

When Boone was 21, he helped the English by fighting in the French and Indian War. Boone fought in the war for a year, and then he returned to North Carolina. In 1756 he married a young woman named Rebecca Bryan. They bought land and farmed it, but Boone still liked to go off to hunt and explore.

In 1763 England finally won the war, and France lost its land in America. England now owned all the land east of the Mississippi River. England made new laws to control the huge area of land. The Proclamation of 1764 forbade colonists to move farther west into Indian lands.

Many colonists ignored the proclamation because they wanted to settle new lands. One of these colonists was Richard Henderson. In 1769 Henderson asked Boone to go west to explore Kentucky. When Boone got there, he was amazed at the Kentucky countryside, with its grassy, rolling hills and forests filled with many animals to hunt and trap. As Boone traveled around, he liked to sing hiking and campfire songs, and he became known for his singing.

In late 1774, Richard Henderson asked Boone to build the Wilderness Road to Kentucky. Henderson planned to buy millions of acres of land from the Indians in Kentucky and then sell the land to colonists for huge profits.

On March 10, 1775, Daniel Boone started the trip with several dozen men. From the Holston River in Tennessee, they went over the Cumberland Gap and headed northwest. They followed animal trails and creek beds, and climbed steep cliffs and mountain ridges. Bushes had to be cut, and trees axed down.

Three weeks later, on April 17, 1775, they ended their 250-mile (400 km) trip at the Kentucky River in the middle of Kentucky. There, they built a new settlement. They named it Boonesborough, and Daniel Boone governed it. Soon, many settlers lived in Boonesborough, including Daniel Boone's own family.

In 1784 a man named John Filson wrote a biography about Daniel Boone. It became a success, and Daniel Boone became a legend. Boone lived into his 80s and continued to hunt, trap, and explore. He died on September 26, 1820, at the age of 85.

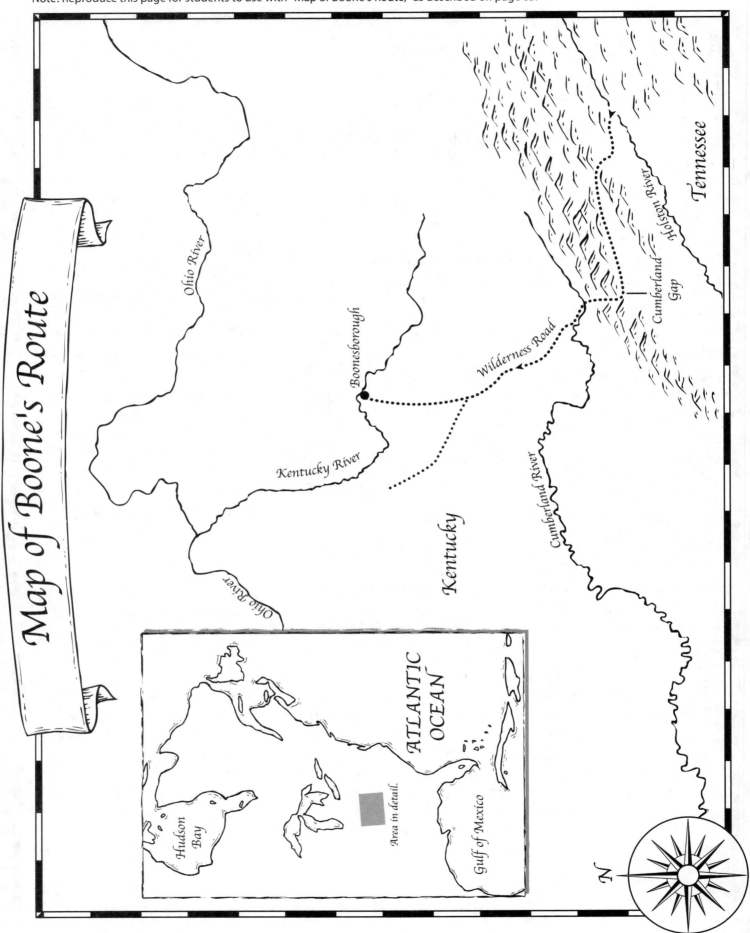

Map of Boone's Route

Ohio River

Boonesborough

Kentucky River

Ohio River

Wilderness Road

Cumberland Gap

Holston River

Cumberland River

Tennessee

Kentucky

ATLANTIC OCEAN

Hudson Bay

Gulf of Mexico

Area in detail.

N

A DANIEL BOONE LIMERICK

Daniel Boone led such a colorful life. Students use colorful, rhyming words to write their own limericks about Daniel Boone.

Here is an example to share with students:

> A hearty frontiersman named Boone
> Could belt out a powerful tune.
> His loud vocal style
> Could carry a mile.
> Critters ran when they heard Daniel croon.

STEPS TO FOLLOW

1. Using the information sheet and fast facts, review the facts about Daniel Boone with students.

2. Read a number of limericks to students so that they get a feel for the rhythm and rhyming pattern.

3. Share the following with students:
   A limerick is one of the most popular of all verse forms in poetry. A limerick is a five-line rhyme with humor and a bouncy rhythm. The rhyme pattern is a–a–b–b–a. Lines 1, 2, and 5 are long rhyming lines; lines 3 and 4 are shorter and also rhyme.

4. Have students write their own limericks.

5. Then have students write a final copy of the limerick on the buckskin jacket pattern.

6. Direct students to color, cut out, and then glue the buckskin jacket to construction paper. Have them cut around it, leaving a border. Students cut the bottom of the shirt to make a fringe border.

7. Encourage students to share their limericks in class.

MATERIALS

- page 68, reproduced for each student
- writing paper
- pencil
- 9" x 12" (23 x 30.5 cm) brown construction paper
- scissors
- crayons or marking pens
- glue

A DANIEL BOONE LIMERICK

(title)

EMC 3708 • Explorers of North America •©2003 by Evan-Moor Corp.

Note: Reproduce this page for students to use with "The Legendary Daniel Boone," as described on page 63.

THE LEGENDARY DANIEL BOONE

A legend is a story from the past whose truth is accepted but cannot be checked.

There is no question that Daniel Boone led an extraordinary life. He had many adventures, some of them extremely dangerous. Because of this, his exploits became legendary.

DIRECTIONS

1. Below are some actual events from Daniel Boone's life. Choose one event and write a legend based on it. Mount your story on a piece of colored contruction paper.

2. Make a cover for your legend. Color, cut out, and glue the picture of Daniel Boone to construction paper. Add a title and additional pictures as desired. Staple the cover to the story.

ACTUAL EVENTS IN BOONE'S LIFE

- Daniel Boone was one of the greatest hunters in America. He named his favorite rifle Tick-Licker.

- Whenever Daniel Boone killed a bear, he would carve an inscription on a tree.

- Daniel Boone was captured four times by Indians. One time the Shawnee chief adopted him into the tribe as his own son. Boone acted as if he loved Indian life while secretly waiting for a chance to escape.

Pocket 9

JAMES
COOK

FAST FACTS

See page 2 for information on how to prepare the Fast Facts bookmark and pocket label. Use the bookmark for a quick review during transition times throughout the day.

ABOUT

Reproduce this page for students. Read and discuss the background information about James Cook, highlighting important information to remember. Incorporate library and multimedia resources that are available.

ACTIVITIES

Reproduce this page for students. Have students locate and color Cook's exploration route on the map. Glue the map onto 9" x 12" (23 x 30.5 cm) construction paper. Place the completed map in the pocket.

Over 400 stamps have been issued worldwide relating to James Cook, his discoveries, and his sailing vessels. Students honor Captain Cook one more time by designing a new stamp and then gluing it to a postcard to send to a friend.

Students study a map of the world and determine if there is a route for the Northwest Passage. Students find out if anyone ever made it through the Northwest Passage.

EMC 3708 • Explorers of North America •©2003 by Evan-Moor Corp.

JAMES COOK

JAMES COOK
FAST FACTS

- Cook was a tough captain. He ordered his men to bathe every day.

- He also ordered his crew to eat onions and pickled cabbage. As a result, none of his men ever died from scurvy.

- He was an accomplished mathematician, astronomer, mapmaker, and surveyor.

- The cottage where Cook lived as a child in England was taken down stone by stone and rebuilt in the public gardens in Melbourne, Australia.

- During a war between England and France, Cook volunteered and was sent to America. He was given the dangerous job of charting the channel of the St. Lawrence River right up to the French lines.

- Once, while working on the river at night, Indians jumped on the back of his boat as he jumped off the front and escaped.

- Cook named the Hawaiian Islands the Sandwich Islands after the Earl of Sandwich—not the food.

- The basic diet for Cook's crew was salted pork and biscuits. Often the food had weevils.

- The *Endeavor* had a goat onboard, so the crew had a little fresh milk to drink. They also brought some pigs and cows that were slaughtered for celebrations.

- James Cook's goal in life was to "Not only go farther than any man had ever been before, but as far as it was possible to go."

ABOUT
JAMES COOK

In 1768 Captain James Cook set off from Plymouth, England. He had 94 people on board his ship, the *Endeavour*. Cook sailed southwest from England and around the lower tip of South America. He headed across the Pacific Ocean to the island of Tahiti.

When they reached Tahiti, Cook and his crew studied the island's plants and animals. They left Tahiti to search for the Southern Continent that the English thought was located on the bottom of the world. He landed in New Zealand and Australia, and made maps of these areas. However, he did not find the Southern Continent. Cook sailed west around the tip of Africa and returned home on July 12, 1771.

In 1772 Cook set off again with two ships, the *Resolution* and the *Adventure*. He had a new navigational tool called a chronometer that would accurately measure longitude. Cook sailed farther south. He reached Antarctica, which was the true Southern Continent.

On July 12, 1776, Cook began his last voyage to find the Northwest Passage. Instead of sailing west, Cook traveled around the lower tip of Africa and continued east to the Pacific Ocean. Cook then headed north and discovered two Hawaiian Islands called Kauai and Niihau. The people on the islands had never seen light-skinned people or large sailing ships. The natives mistook Cook for a peaceful god called Lono.

Cook spent over a month in Hawai`i, exploring and mapping the islands. When he left Hawai`i, Cook headed north to find the Northwest Passage. He sailed along the shores of Canada and Alaska. When Cook finally reached the Arctic Ocean, ice made him turn back. He did not find a Northwest Passage and headed south toward warmer weather.

In 1778 Cook returned to the Hawaiian Islands. A disagreement with the natives over a stolen boat turned violent and Cook died in the fight. Cook's sad crew had to sail back to England without him.

Cook provided records of the many cultures he had met during his voyages. He had also made accurate charts and maps of the regions he visited.

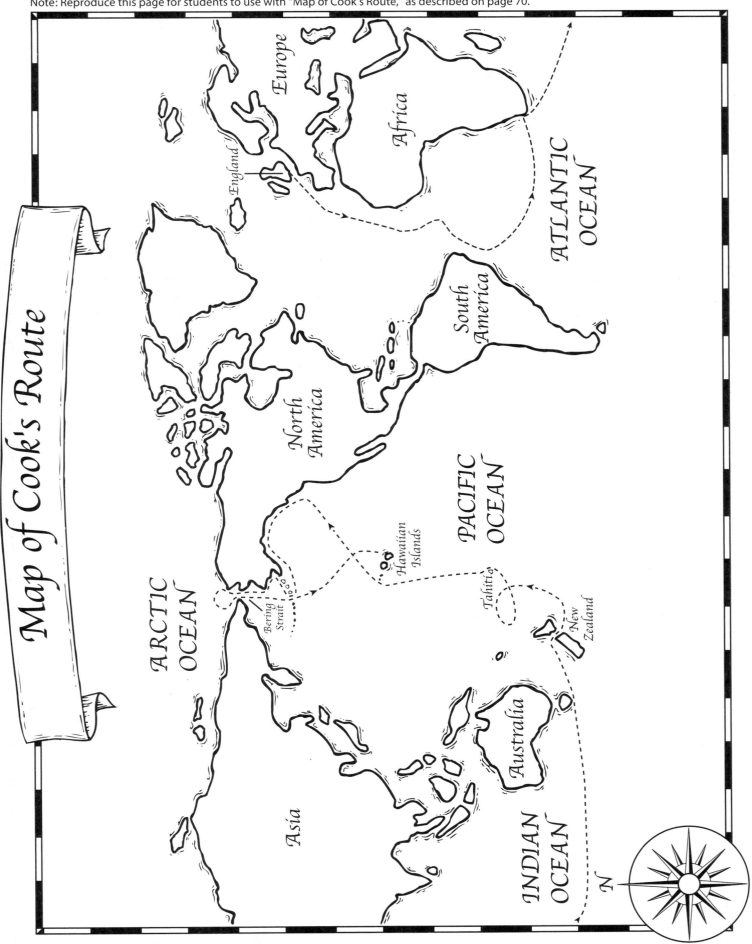

Map of Cook's Route

Europe

Africa

England

ATLANTIC OCEAN

South America

North America

PACIFIC OCEAN

Hawaiian Islands

Tahiti

New Zealand

ARCTIC OCEAN

Bering Strait

Australia

Asia

INDIAN OCEAN

N

MATERIALS

- page 75, reproduced for each student
- 9" x 12" (23 x 30.5 cm) construction paper
- pencil
- crayons or marking pens
- scissors
- glue

ONE MORE STAMP

Students make just one more stamp to commemorate this great explorer. Have them glue it to a postcard and then "send" it to a friend.

STEPS TO FOLLOW

1. Hand out page 75 to students. Read the information about James Cook together.

2. Have students design and decorate a stamp for Captain James Cook. Direct them to include a picture that represents him in some way, his name, and the dates 1728–1778.

3. Have students cut out the stamp and glue it to the postcard on page 75.

4. Students then write a postcard to a friend telling a little something about James Cook. Students address the postcard.

5. Instruct students to cut out the postcard and glue it to construction paper. They trim around it to make a border.

6. Have students "send" their postcards to friends in class.

EMC 3708 • Explorers of North America • ©2003 by Evan-Moor Corp.

ONE MORE STAMP

Affix
Postage
Here

*O*ver 400 stamps have been issued worldwide relating to Captain James Cook. The stamps represent all three of his voyages and his discoveries. The stamps include pictures of him and pictures of his three sailing ships (the *Endeavour, Resolution,* and *Adventure*). The stamps also represent some plants, animals, and native peoples he and his crew studied in Hawai`i, Tahiti, New Zealand, and Australia. There are stamps dedicated to the scientists' observations of Venus when they sailed with Cook in 1769. The stamps also depict his voyage in the Arctic region trying to find the Northwest Passage.

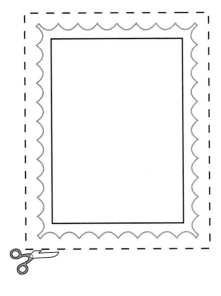

IS THERE REALLY A NORTHWEST PASSAGE?

The Spanish, the British, and the French all wanted to reach the riches of the East by sailing west. Students learn that Roald Amundsen finally found the Northwest Passage after Cartier, Hudson, and Cook had all failed.

Students use a map to trace the Northwest Passage route, following the teacher's oral directions.

MATERIALS

- map showing North America and the Arctic
- page 77, reproduced for each student
- pencil
- colored pencils

STEPS TO FOLLOW

1. Recall how three of the explorers that the students studied—Cartier, Hudson, and Cook—had tried finding the Northwest Passage and how they had all failed.

2. Hand out copies of the map on page 77. Have students look at the map while individuals read aloud the passage about Amundsen's route.

3. Direct students to trace Amundsen's route with a pencil as you read the passage again slowly.

4. Using a large map of North America and the Arctic, trace the route and discuss how close the students came to the actual route. Have them make corrections on their map, if needed.

5. Encourage students to color the map.

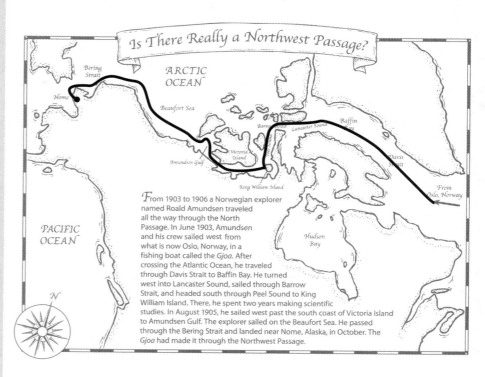

Is There Really a Northwest Passage?

From 1903 to 1906 a Norwegian explorer named Roald Amundsen traveled all the way through the North Passage. In June 1903, Amundsen and his crew sailed west from what is now Oslo, Norway, in a fishing boat called the *Gjoa*. After crossing the Atlantic Ocean, he traveled through Davis Strait to Baffin Bay. He turned west into Lancaster Sound, sailed through Barrow Strait, and headed south through Peel Sound to King William Island. There, he spent two years making scientific studies. In August 1905, he sailed west past the south coast of Victoria Island to Amundsen Gulf. The explorer sailed on the Beaufort Sea. He passed through the Bering Strait and landed near Nome, Alaska, in October. The *Gjoa* had made it through the Northwest Passage.

EMC 3708 • Explorers of North America •©2003 by Evan-Moor Corp.

Is There Really a Northwest Passage?

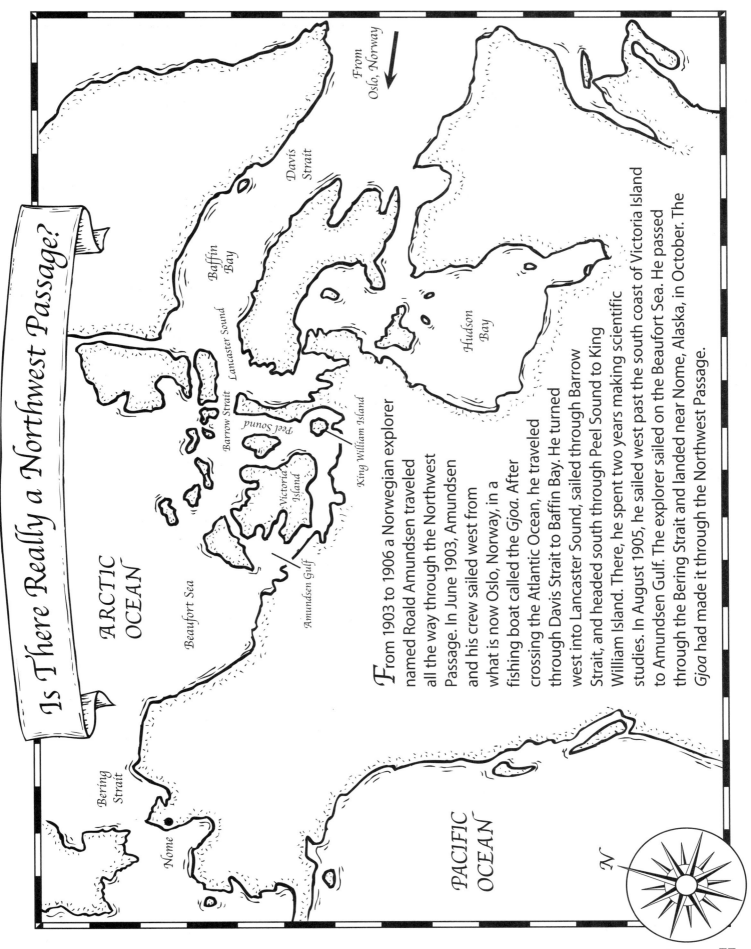

ARCTIC OCEAN

PACIFIC OCEAN

Beaufort Sea

Bering Strait

Nome

Amundsen Gulf

Victoria Island

Peel Sound

Barrow Strait

King William Island

Lancaster Sound

Baffin Bay

Davis Strait

Hudson Bay

From Oslo, Norway

N

From 1903 to 1906 a Norwegian explorer named Roald Amundsen traveled all the way through the Northwest Passage. In June 1903, Amundsen and his crew sailed west from what is now Oslo, Norway, in a fishing boat called the *Gjoa*. After crossing the Atlantic Ocean, he traveled through Davis Strait to Baffin Bay. He turned west into Lancaster Sound, sailed through Barrow Strait, and headed south through Peel Sound to King William Island. There, he spent two years making scientific studies. In August 1905, he sailed west past the south coast of Victoria Island. He passed to Amundsen Gulf. The explorer sailed on the Beaufort Sea. He passed through the Bering Strait and landed near Nome, Alaska, in October. The *Gjoa* had made it through the Northwest Passage.

Pocket 10

LEWIS AND CLARK

FAST FACTS

Lewis and Clark . . . . **page 79**
See page 2 for information on how to prepare the Fast Facts bookmark and pocket label. Use the bookmark for a quick review during transition times throughout the day.

ABOUT

Lewis and Clark . . . . **page 80**
Reproduce this page for students. Read and discuss the background information about Lewis and Clark, highlighting important information to remember. Incorporate library and multimedia resources that are available.

ACTIVITIES

Map of Lewis and Clark's Route . . . . **page 81**
Reproduce this page for students. Have students locate and color Lewis and Clark's exploration route on the map. Glue the map onto 9" x 12" (23 x 30.5 cm) construction paper. Place the completed map in the pocket.

Exploration Journals . . . . **pages 82 & 83**
Lewis and Clark kept journals on their journey. They recorded observations and included drawings of the plant and animal life. Students make observation journals, then write and draw in them for a week.

Newspaper Moccasins . . . . **pages 84 & 85**
Students make moccasins from folded newspaper or brown wrapping paper, and imagine what it would have been like for the Corps of Discovery to walk many miles through prickly pears, on hard rocks, and through rivers.

EMC 3708 • Explorers of North America •©2003 by Evan-Moor Corp.

LEWIS AND CLARK

FAST FACTS

- Clark was in charge of recruiting the men, and Lewis was in charge of gathering the equipment.

- Lewis had a broad knowledge of native plants and animals.

- Lewis was 28 when the expedition began. Clark was 32.

- Lewis took a Newfoundland dog, Seaman, with him on the expedition.

- Appendicitis caused the only death on the expedition.

- During the winter at Fort Mandan, the Corps traded tools for the Indian's crops of corn, melons, and beans.

- Lewis's journal tells of "immence herds of Buffaloe, Elk, Deer, & Antelopes feeding in one common and boundless pasture."

- The men of the Corps hunted grizzly bears on occasion. Lewis commented that he would "reather fight two Indians than one bear."

- Another tribe had captured Sacagawea as a young girl. When the Corps reached Shoshone lands, she was reunited with her brother, now a chief.

- In Idaho, a Nez Perce tribe entertained the Corps with a feast of salmon, berries, and roots. The explorers became quite ill from this unfamiliar food.

- When the Corps reached the Pacific Ocean, they voted on which side of the Columbia River to stay on. This historical event included the vote of a woman, Sacagawea, and a black man, York.

ABOUT
LEWIS AND CLARK

Thomas Jefferson was president of the United States when the Louisiana Territory was purchased from France in 1803. This purchase doubled the size of the United States. Jefferson wanted to explore this new territory, and he also wanted to see if there was a Northwest Passage from the Mississippi River to the Pacific Ocean that would lead to the Indies.

To lead the expedition, Jefferson hired his secretary, Meriwether Lewis, who was a former army officer. Lewis asked his former army commander, William Clark, to be his partner. They spent time gathering supplies and hiring people to join their group called the Corps of Discovery.

On May 14, 1804, Lewis and Clark and about 40 other men set off in three boats from near St. Louis, Missouri, where the Missouri River flows into the Mississippi River. They traveled northwest up the Missouri River. Lewis and Clark drew maps and kept detailed journals of the areas they traveled.

When they reached South Dakota in September, they fought with Teton Sioux Indians. In October, they were in North Dakota and spent the winter with a tribe of friendly natives called Mandans. They met a French-Canadian fur trader named Toussaint Charbonneau. He had a young wife named Sacagawea, who was a Shoshone Indian. Lewis and Clark hired Charbonneau and Sacagawea as guides and interpreters.

In April 1805, the group headed west toward Montana. When they came to rapidly flowing water, they had to carry the boats on land for miles. In August, Sacagawea recognized familiar land. The expedition finally met up with a tribe of Shoshones, and the leader was Sacagawea's brother. The Shoshones provided the Corps of Discovery with horses and a Shoshone guide.

In September, they crossed over the Bitterroot Mountains into Idaho. They continued west along the Columbia River and finally reached the Pacific Ocean in November 1805. In northern Oregon, they built a fort called Fort Clatsop and spent the winter there.

The Corps of Discovery returned to St. Louis on September 3, 1806. They had traveled a total of 9,000 miles (14,484 km) in a year and a half. Lewis and Clark provided accurate maps and journals of the areas they visited. Many settlers followed the Lewis and Clark Trail to the West. They had found a rich new land for the new country.

   EMC 3708 • Explorers of North America •©2003 by Evan-Moor Corp.

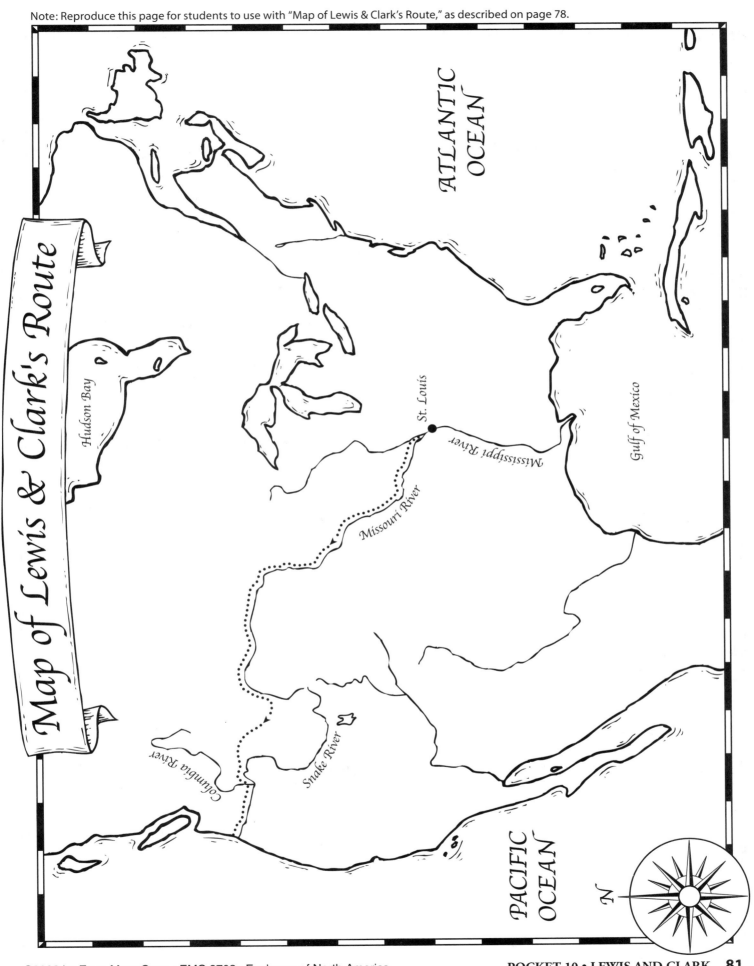

Map of Lewis & Clark's Route

POCKET 10 • LEWIS AND CLARK

ATLANTIC OCEAN

Hudson Bay

St. Louis

Mississippi River

Missouri River

Gulf of Mexico

Columbia River

Snake River

PACIFIC OCEAN

N

MATERIALS

- page 83, one front cover and five journal pages reproduced for each student
- two 6" x 9" (15 x 23 cm) pieces of light brown construction paper
- two 15" (38 cm) pieces of ribbon or yarn
- glue
- colored pencils or crayons
- pencil or pen
- hole punch
- stapler
- scissors

EXPLORATION JOURNALS

Meriwether Lewis kept accurate and detailed journals on the exploration through the United States. Those journals inspired people to move west.

Students make their own exploration journals, and then write and draw in them for a week.

STEPS TO FOLLOW

1. Recall how Lewis and Clark kept journals of their trip. They wrote about the plants, animals, and people they saw along their journey of exploration. They also sketched pictures. We know a lot about what happened during the travels of the Corps of Discovery because of these journals.

2. Tell students they get to make their own journals. Pass out the cover and journal pages on page 83 and two pieces of construction paper.

3. Students write their name on the front cover. They color, cut out, and glue the cover to one piece of construction paper.

4. Have students cut out the journal pages and staple them to the other piece of construction paper. Hole punch front and back covers. Put the journal together by lacing yarn through the holes.

5. Have students explore the school grounds. They carry their journal with them for five days during a time determined by you. They should write down everything they see, hear, and do.

6. Students then share their journals with the class.

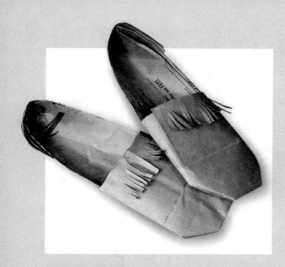

PAPER MOCCASINS

Students make folded moccasins from large brown paper bags and imagine what it would have been like for the Corps of Discovery to walk many miles through prickly pears, on hard rocks, and through rivers.

STEPS TO FOLLOW

1. Tell students that people in the Lewis and Clark expedition wore moccasins later in the journey when their shoes gave out. The moccasins were made of elk skin.

2. Instruct students in how to make moccasins following the directions below.

3. Distribute a copy of page 85 to each student. Read the journal entries with students. Mention that Lewis and Clark had their own ways to spell words, although for the most part we can tell what they say. Explain that the prickly pear is a type of cactus.

4. Ask students to put on their moccasins and take a walk outside. Have them walk over different surfaces.

5. When they get back from their walk, have students describe what it felt like to walk a long way in their moccasins.

HOW TO MAKE PAPER MOCCASINS

1. Cut open a paper bag so it lays flat.

2. Measure the bag as shown. Then cut off the bottom and top sections of the bag.

3. Fold down the top 6" (15 cm) as shown.

4. Divide the paper into thirds and fold the two side panels to the back.

5. Turn it over and tuck one folded corner under the flap of the other folded corner, and tape to secure in place.

6. Slip your foot into the pocket. Keeping your foot flat on the ground, pull up the sides along the edges of your foot. Then shape the sole of the moccasin around your heel.

7. Pinch the end of the paper at the back of your heel so the moccasin comes to a point. Pull the paper end that extends beyond your heel around to the inner side of your foot and tape it.

8. Repeat with the second bag to make the other moccasin.

9. Cut fringe from paper bag scraps and glue it to the moccasins.

MATERIALS

- page 85, reproduced for each student
- two large brown paper bags, for each student
- tape
- scissors
- pencil
- ruler
- glue

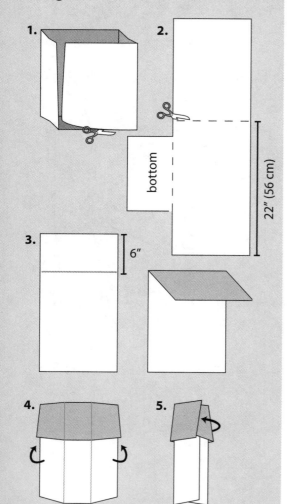

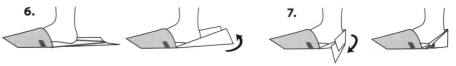

EMC 3708 • Explorers of North America •©2003 by Evan-Moor Corp.

LEWIS AND CLARK JOURNAL ENTRIES
ABOUT MOCCASINS AND SORE FEET

August 4, 1805:
    They are obliged to drag the canoes over the stone there not being water enough to float them...and being unable to walk on the shore for the brush wade in the river along the shore and hawl them by the cord; this has increased the pain and labour extreemly; their feet soon get tender and soar by wading and walking over the stones.

—Meriwether Lewis

June 22, 1805:
The prickly pears were extreemly troublesome to us sticking our feet through our mockersons.

—Meriwether Lewis

June 23, 1805:
This evening the men repaired their mockersons, and put on double souls to protect their feet from the prickly pears. During the late rains the buffaloe have troden up the praire very much which having now become dry the sharp points of earth as hard as frozen ground stand up in such abundance that there is no avoiding them. This is particular severe on the feet of the men...some are limping from the soreness of their feet...yet no one complains, all go with cheerfulness.

—Meriwether Lewis

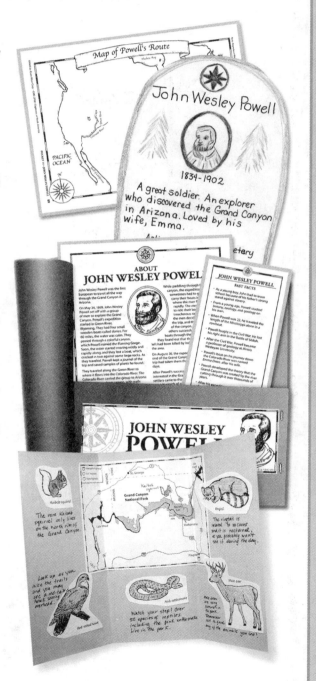

Pocket 11

JOHN WESLEY POWELL

FAST FACTS

See page 2 for information on how to prepare the Fast Facts bookmark and pocket label. Use the bookmark for a quick review during transition times throughout the day.

ABOUT

Reproduce this page for students. Read and discuss the background information about John Wesley Powell, highlighting important information to remember. Incorporate library and multimedia resources that are available.

ACTIVITIES

Reproduce this page for students. Have students locate and color Powell's exploration route on the map. Glue the map onto 9" x 12" (23 x 30.5 cm) construction paper. Place the completed map in the pocket.

Major John Wesley Powell is buried in the National Cemetery in Arlington, Virginia. His epitaph is short and simple, but respectful. Students write a new inscription honoring this great major and explorer.

John Wesley Powell could never have imagined that 5 million people would visit the Grand Canyon National Park every year. Students read about this national treasure and then make a new brochure for park visitors.

JOHN WESLEY POWELL

FAST FACTS

- As a young boy, John had to leave school because of his father's strong stand against slavery.

- From a young age, Powell studied botany, zoology, and geology on his own.

- When Powell was 22, he traveled the length of the Mississippi alone in a rowboat.

- Powell fought in the Civil War. He lost his right arm in the Battle of Shiloh.

- After the Civil War, Powell became a professor of geology at Illinois Wesleyan University.

- Powell's boat on his journey down the Colorado River was named *Emma Dean,* after his wife.

- Powell developed the theory that the Grand Canyon was created by the river cutting through it over thousands of years.

- After his expedition down the Colorado, Powell became a national hero.

- John Wesley Powell is buried in Arlington National Cemetery near Washington, D.C.

ABOUT
JOHN WESLEY POWELL

John Wesley Powell was the first European to travel all the way through the Grand Canyon in Arizona.

On May 24, 1869, John Wesley Powell set off with a group of men to explore the Grand Canyon. Powell's expedition started in Green River, Wyoming. They had four small wooden boats called dories. For 60 miles, the water was calm. They passed through a colorful canyon, which Powell named the Flaming Gorge. Soon, the water started moving wildly and rapidly along, and they lost a boat, which cracked in two against some large rocks. As they traveled, Powell kept a journal of the trip and saved samples of plants he found.

They traveled along the Green River to where it flows into the Colorado River. The Colorado River carried the group to Arizona and into a very deep canyon, with walls about 5,000 feet (1,524 m) high. This was the beginning of the Grand Canyon. Powell named most of the features in the canyon, including Bright Angel Creek and Vasey's Paradise.

While paddling through the canyon, the expedition sometimes had to get out and carry their boats in places where the river flowed too rapidly. The men also had to ride their boats through treacherous rapids. Three of the men decided to abandon the trip, and they climbed out of the canyon. Powell and the others successfully rode their boats through the rapids. Later, they found out that the three men who left had been killed by Indians who lived in the area.

On August 30, the expedition reached the end of the Grand Canyon. The 1,000-mile trip had taken them three months and six days.

After Powell's successful trip, people became interested in the Grand Canyon. More white settlers came to the area. Some people came in search of gold, but found copper instead. In 1919 the Grand Canyon became a national park.

 EMC 3708 • Explorers of North America •©2003 by Evan-Moor Corp.

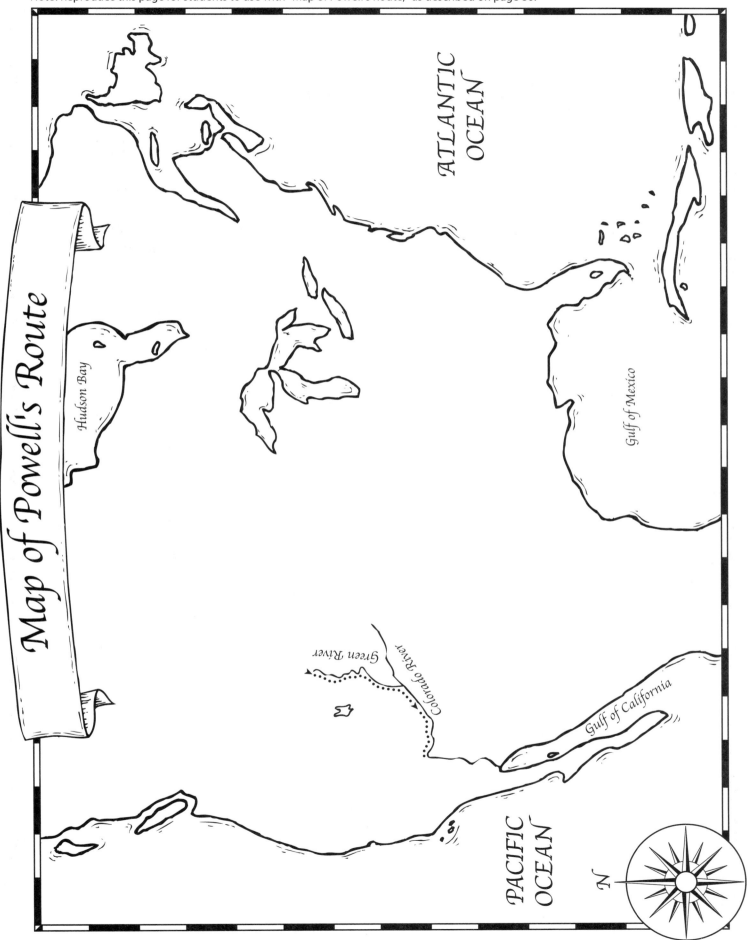

Map of Powell's Route

ATLANTIC OCEAN

Hudson Bay

Gulf of Mexico

Green River

Colorado River

Gulf of California

PACIFIC OCEAN

N

MATERIALS

- 9" x 12" (23 x 30.5 cm) light-colored construction paper
- pencil
- crayons or marking pens
- scissors

POWELL'S EPITAPH

Students write a new epitaph for Powell to honor this great major and explorer.

Major John Wesley Powell was honored by being buried in the National Cemetery in Arlington, Virginia. His wife, Emma, was buried alongside him. On his gravestone, there is a picture of him and an epitaph. An epitaph is an inscription on a tomb or gravestone in memory of the person buried there. Powell's epitaph is short and simple, but respectful. His tombstone reads:

STEPS TO FOLLOW

1. Write the epitaph written about John Wesley Powell on the chalkboard, and discuss his accomplishments in life. Refer back to the fast facts and information pages for his accomplishments.

2. Discuss the fact that inscriptions or epitaphs were common on tombstones in the 1800s and 1900s.

3. Have students write a new respectful epitaph for Powell, highlighting an important accomplishment in his life.

4. Direct them to make an outline of a gravestone marker on the construction paper.

5. Then they write the epitaph on the construction paper. They should also include a picture of him or some important part of his life, his name, and the dates 1834–1902.

6. Instruct students to cut out their markers and share the epitaphs of John Wesley Powell with the class.

EMC 3708 • Explorers of North America • ©2003 by Evan-Moor Corp.

GRAND CANYON VISITOR'S GUIDE

Students make a new brochure for the Grand Canyon National Park.

"Do nothing to mar its grandeur for the ages have been at work upon it and man cannot improve it. Keep it for your children, your children's children, and all who come after you...."

—Theodore Roosevelt

Roosevelt's words about the Grand Canyon and its preservation ring true today. John Wesley Powell could not have ever imagined that today 5 million people visit the Grand Canyon National Park every year.

STEPS TO FOLLOW

1. Discuss the information and map of the Grand Canyon National Park given on pages 92 and 93. Use other reference materials on the Grand Canyon, if available. (For more information, write to Superintendent, P.O. Box 129, Grand Canyon, AZ 86023–0129.)

2. Tell students that the park officials want a new design for a brochure to attract visitors to the park, and they have been assigned to do the job.

3. Show students how to fold the construction paper into thirds. This will give them six panels. You may want the students to make a "mock up" of the brochure before they complete a final copy.

4. Share ideas for the six panels with the students. Ideas include a front cover with the title, statistics about the park, attractions to see, modes of transportation, a map of the area or of Arizona, pictures of the animals, the Colorado River, a slogan or Theodore Roosevelt's words, and information about John Wesley Powell.

5. Have students design and then color their new brochures for the park. You may choose to have students cut and paste the information, map, and pictures on pages 92 and 93 instead of drawing them.

MATERIALS

- pages 92 and 93, reproduced for each student
- 9" x 12" (23 x 30.5 cm) white construction paper
- pencil
- crayons or marking pens
- scissors
- glue
- reference materials on the Grand Canyon, if available

GRAND CANYON VISITOR'S GUIDE

Grand Canyon Facts

- The Grand Canyon is considered one of the Seven Natural Wonders of the World.

- The Grand Canyon National Park includes over 1,000,000 acres (493,077 ha) of land.

- The Colorado River runs along the base of the canyon. The river formed the canyon millions of years ago.

- The rock layers of the canyon vary in shade and color. Shades of red, yellow, brown, and green are seen on the canyon walls.

- The highest point on the North Rim of the canyon is about 9,000 feet (2,743 m) above sea level.

- In some places the gorge of the canyon is one mile (1.6 km) deep and up to 18 miles (29 km) wide.

- A trip to the bottom of the canyon on foot or by mule is a whole day's journey.

- The Havasupai Indians live in the inner canyon of the Grand Canyon. Their village can only be reached by foot, pack animal, or from the river.

Colorado River

Grand Canyon National Park

Animals of the Grand Canyon

- There are 75 species of mammals and 50 species of reptiles and amphibians that live in the Grand Canyon. There are also some 300 species of birds found there.

- Mule deer are the most common mammal in the park.

- Bighorn sheep can be found on the slopes of the inner canyon.

- Bobcats, coyotes, and a small population of mountain lions roam the park.

- Smaller mammals include ringtails, beavers, gophers, chipmunks, squirrels, rabbits, and bats.

- There are many kinds of lizards, snakes, turtles, frogs, toads, and salamanders throughout the park.

- The unique pink rattlesnakes and the white-tailed Kaibab squirrels are only found in the Grand Canyon.

- Peregrine falcons, bald eagles, and red-tailed hawks fly above the canyon walls.

Red-tailed hawk

   EMC 3708 • Explorers of North America •©2003 by Evan-Moor Corp.

GRAND CANYON VISITOR'S GUIDE

Red-tailed hawk

Kaibab squirrel

Mule deer

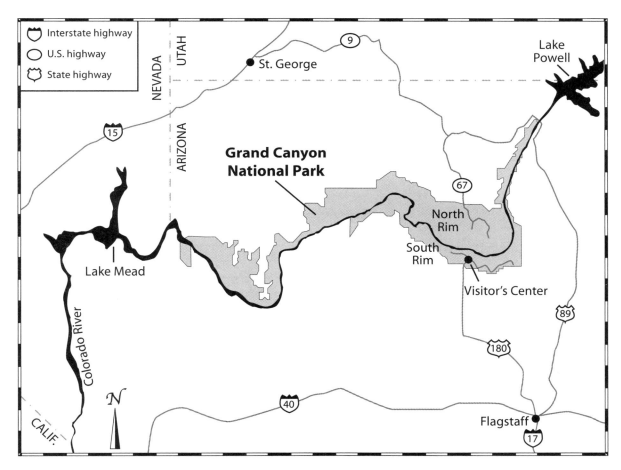

Interstate highway
U.S. highway
State highway

NEVADA
UTAH
ARIZONA
CALIF.

St. George
9
Lake Powell
15
Grand Canyon National Park
67
North Rim
South Rim
Visitor's Center
Lake Mead
Colorado River
89
180
40
Flagstaff
17
N

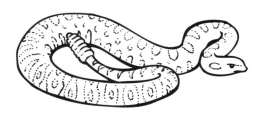

Pink rattlesnake

Ringtail

Explorer Job Application Form

Now that you have learned about several different explorers, it is time for you to choose which one you would have wanted to join on his expedition. After you have made your choice, fill out the job application to convince your explorer you are highly qualified to become an explorer.

Name _____ Date _____

Address _____

City _____ State _____ Zip Code _____

I want to join _____ on his exploration of

_____

The reason I want to go on this exploration is to _____

_____

_____

Educational Background _____

_____

_____

Work Experience _____

_____

_____

_____

Special Skills _____

_____

_____

_____

Signature _____

EXPLORERS OF NORTH AMERICA—REFLECTION SHEET

Name: _____ Date: _____

Directions: Please fill out this sheet after you have completed the Explorers of North America book. Place your reflection sheet in the first pocket.

1. When I look through my Explorers of North America book, I feel _____

   because _____

   _____

2. The project I liked doing the most was the _____

   because _____

   _____

3. The project I liked doing the least was the _____

   because _____

   _____

4. Three things I am most proud of in my Explorers of North America book are _____

   _____

   _____

   _____

5. Three things I would do differently to improve my Explorers of North America book are _____

   _____

   _____

   _____

6. Three facts that I learned about Explorers of North America that I did not know before doing this

   project are _____

   _____

   _____

7. The explorer that was the most interesting to me was _____

   because _____

   _____

   _____

EXPLORERS OF NORTH AMERICA—REFLECTION SHEET

Directions: Look through all the pockets and evaluate how well the activities were completed. Use the following point system:

6 outstanding	5 excellent	4 very good	3 satisfactory	2 some effort	1 little effort	0 no effort

Self-Evaluation	Peer Evaluation	Teacher Evaluation
Name: _____	Name: _____	____ completed assignments
____ completed assignments	____ completed assignments	____ followed directions
____ followed directions	____ followed directions	____ had correct information
____ had correct information	____ had correct information	____ edited writing
____ edited writing	____ edited writing	____ showed creativity
____ showed creativity	____ showed creativity	____ displayed neatness
____ displayed neatness	____ displayed neatness	____ added color
____ added color	____ added color	____ **total points**
____ **total points**	____ **total points**	____ **grade**
Comments: _____	Comments: _____	Comments: _____